The Interpretation
of Scripture

The Interpretation of Scripture

In Defense of the Historical-Critical Method

Joseph A. Fitzmyer, S.J.

PAULIST PRESS
New York/Mahwah, N.J.

The Scripture quotations contained herein are the author's own translation.

Cover design by Tim McKeen
Book design by Lynn Else

Library of Congress Cataloging-in-Publication Data

Fitzmyer, Joseph A.
    The interpretation of Scripture : in defense of the historical-critical method / Joseph A. Fitzmyer.
        p. cm.
    Includes bibliographical references (p.   ) and indexes.
    ISBN 978-0-8091-4504-1
    1. Bible—Criticism, interpretation, etc. 2. Catholic Church—Doctrines. I. Title.
    BS531.F58 2008
    220.601—dc22

                                                                            2007036897

Published by Paulist Press
997 Macarthur Boulevard
Mahwah, New Jersey 07430

www.paulistpress.com

Printed and bound in the
United States of America

CONTENTS

PREFACE

This collection of essays on the interpretation of Scripture is made up of the revision of a number of articles published since 1961 on issues that arose in the intervening decades about modes of interpreting the Bible in the Church. In one way or another, these essays reveal how the Bible is understood there today, or better, how it has come to be read by Catholic laity, pastors, theologians, and biblical scholars. The path that such a reading of Scripture traversed has been beset by controversies and at times by willful misunderstanding. Many of the controversies no longer exist, thank Heavens, but they should not be allowed to pass into oblivion, because the lessons learned from them may prevent the recurrence of them.

The lessons are needed today among Catholics, but also among non-Catholics, who may encounter similar problems in their own Churches, where a fundamentalistic reading of the Bible has the potential to cause trouble, or where the historical-critical method of interpretation has been found suspect.

The incentive to revise these essays came from a collection of various articles of mine that John R. Donahue, S.J., made for a course that he was to give on the interpretation of Scripture at the Jesuit School of Theology in Berkeley, California. He gathered them together and scanned them, producing the collection on a CD. In giving me a copy of it, he suggested that I might consider revising and updating the articles. This I have tried to do, and the result is the collection of essays now being published in this book. Needless to say, I am very grateful to him for all the work he did in assembling the collection. Some of the articles that he chose did not really suit the topic of this book, and I have not included them. Donahue also agreed to read through the manuscript of this book and comment on it in the revised form; I am therefore doubly grateful to him for this courteous assistance.

My thanks are also due to a number of persons who have helped me in the preparation of the manuscript for this book, such the Rev. J. Leon Hooper, S.J., director of the Woodstock Theological Center Library, housed here at Georgetown University, and his capable staff, who assisted me in the acquisition of a number of items not easily found. I am also grateful to the Rev. Michael P. Kerrigan, C.S.P., for his careful editing of the text to make it a book that Paulist Press publishes.

Joseph A. Fitzmyer, S.J.
Professor Emeritus, Biblical Studies
The Catholic University of America
Resident at the Jesuit Community
Georgetown University
Washington, DC 20057-1200

ACKNOWLEDGMENTS

Essay 1 appeared under the same title that it bears here in *Faith, Word and Culture* (ed. Liam Bergin; Blackrock, Co. Dublin: Columba Press, 2004) 32–50.

Essay 2 appeared originally as "A Recent Roman Scriptural Controversy," *TS* 22 (1961) 426–44.

Essay 3 appeared under the same title in *TS* 25 (1964) 386–408.

Essay 4 appeared under the same title in *TS* 50 (1989) 244–59.

Essay 5 appeared under the same title in *Josephinum Journal of Theology* 6 (1999) 5–20.

Essay 6 is a reduced combination of two articles, "Problems of the Literal and Spiritual Senses of Scripture," *Louvain Studies* 20 (1995) 134–46, and "The Senses of Scripture Today," *Irish Theological Quarterly* 62 (1996–97) 101–17.

Essay 7 appeared originally as "Raymond E. Brown, S.S. In Memoriam," in *Union Seminary Quarterly Review* 52 (1998) 1–18.

The author is grateful to the editors of these publications for permission to use and revise them for this collection.

ABBREVIATIONS

AAS	*Acta Apostolicae Sedis*
AB	Anchor Bible
ABD	Freedman, D. N. (ed.), *Anchor Bible Dictionary* (6 vols.; New York: Doubleday, 1992)
ABRL	Anchor Bible Reference Library
AER	*American Ecclesiastical Review*
ASS	*Acta Sanctae Sedis*
Bib	*Biblica*
BTB	*Biblical Theology Bulletin*
BZ	*Biblische Zeitschrift*
CBQ	*Catholic Biblical Quarterly*
CSEL	*Corpus Scriptorum Ecclesiasticorum Latinorum*
DaS	Pope Pius XII, *Divino afflante Spiritu* (Encyclical of 1943)
DBSup	Pirot, L., et al. (eds.), *Dictionnaire de la Bible, Supplement* (13 vols. to date; Paris: Letouzey & Ané, 1928–2005)
DH	Denzinger, H., and P. Hünermann, *Enchiridion symbolorum definitionum et declarationum de rebus fidei et morum* (37th ed.; Freiburg im B.: Herder, 1991)
EB	*Enchiridion Biblicum: Documenti della Chiesa sulla Sacra Scrittura, Edizione bilingue* (Bologna: Edizioni Dehoniane, 1993)
ESBNT	Fitzmyer, J. A., *Essays on the Semitic Background of the New Testament* (London: G. Chapman, 1971; repr. Missoula, MT: Scholars Press, 1974)
ETL	*Ephemerides Theologicae Lovanienses*
GCS	*Griechische christliche Schriftsteller*
IDBSup	Crim, K. (ed.), *The Interpreter's Dictionary of the Bible, Supplementary Volume* (Nashville, TN: Abingdon, 1976)

JBC   Brown, R. E., et al. (eds.), *The Jerome Biblical Commentary* (Englewood Cliffs, NJ: Prentice Hall, 1968)

JBL   *Journal of Biblical Literature*

JSOTSup   Supplements to the *Journal for the Study of the Old Testament*

LXX   Septuagint

NJBC   Brown, R. E., et al. (eds.), *The New Jerome Biblical Commentary* (Englewood Cliffs, NJ: Prentice Hall, 1990)

NT   New Testament

NTA   *New Testament Abstracts*

OT   Old Testament

PG   Migne, J. (ed.), *Patrologia Graeca*

PL   Migne, J. (ed.), *Patrologia Latina*

QD   Quaestiones Disputatae

RB   *Revue Biblique*

RHE   *Revue de l'Histoire Ecclésiastique*

RSR   *Recherches de Science Religieuse*

SBNT   Fitzmyer, J. A., *The Semitic Background of the New Testament* (Grand Rapids, MI: Eerdmans; Livonia, MI: Dove Booksellers, 1997); see *ESBNT*

SC   *Sources Chrétiennes*

SD   Béchard, D. P. (ed.), *The Scripture Documents: An Anthology of Official Catholic Teachings* (Collegeville, MN: Liturgical Press, 2002)

S.T.   *Thomas Aquinas, Summa Theologiae*

TS   *Theological Studies*

VDom   *Verbum Domini*

1

THE SECOND VATICAN COUNCIL AND THE ROLE OF THE BIBLE IN CATHOLIC LIFE

The Catholic Church has experienced a remarkable return to the Bible in recent decades. Catholic people, lay persons, theologians, and biblical scholars, have been devoting their time and energy not only to prayer that is biblically oriented, but also to the study of the Bible. This has not always been true in the centuries prior to the mid-twentieth century, especially since the time of the Reformation. Then reformers such as Martin Luther and John Calvin emphasized the study of the written Word of God in a new way and insisted on the instruction and education of the faithful in an area that had become somewhat neglected.

Part of the unfortunate heritage of the Counter Reformation has been that Catholics tended to shy away from the Bible, as if it were "the Protestant book." In doing so, they lost in the post-Tridentine era much of their own Christian heritage, for Sacred Scripture had been a vital influence in Christian life in the patristic and medieval periods and was acquiring a new emphasis at the time of the Renaissance with its stress on *recursus ad fontes* (getting back to the sources). With those new developments in the fourteenth, fifteenth, and early sixteenth centuries, numerous Catholic scholars were in the forefront of the study of the Bible and the languages in which it was originally composed, Hebrew, Aramaic, and Greek, even though the ordinary people were not well instructed in biblical teaching or the contents of the Bible.

In the post-Tridentine era, when Jansenism plagued the life of the Church in the seventeenth and eighteenth century, Pope Clement XI issued a Constitution, *Unigenitus Dei Filius*, which censured 101 propositions of the Frenchman Pasquier Quesnel, one of the leaders

1

of the Jansenist movement. The propositions were said to be "false, captious, badly worded, offensive to pious ears, scandalous,…blasphemous,…and close to heresy… (§101).[1] Among the propositions were several that dealt with the Bible, and from them one gains an impression of how the Bible was regarded then in Catholic life. Toward the end of the seventeenth century, Quesnel had published a book entitled *Le Nouveau Testament en français avec des réflexions morales sur chaque verset* (1693). When he commented on the story of the Ethiopian eunuch who was returning home from a visit to Jerusalem and reading the fifty-third chapter of the prophet Isaiah in his carriage (Acts 8:28), Quesnel wrote, "The reading of Sacred Scripture is for everybody." Obviously, Quesnel thought that, if Scripture itself depicts an Ethiopian eunuch reading Isaiah, then everybody should read Scripture. That proposition, however, fell under papal censure in Clement XI's document (§80).[2] We would love to know what in it was "offensive to pious ears" or "close to heresy." Another censured proposition was: "The holy obscurity of the Word of God is not a reason for the laity to dispense themselves from the reading of it" (§81).[3] That was Quesnel's moral reflection on Acts 8:31, which records the Ethiopian's question, "How can I (understand Isaiah), unless someone guides me?" Still another censured proposition was: "Sunday ought to be kept holy by pious readings and above all by the reading of Sacred Scriptures. It is damnably wrong to want to withhold a Christian from such reading" (§82), a comment on Acts 15:21, where Luke depicts James of Jerusalem saying that Moses is read every sabbath in the synagogue. I cite these censured propositions to make us aware in the twenty-first century how Catholics often lived their lives almost independently of the Bible in the post-Tridentine era. Pope Clement XI obviously had good reason to censure many of the Jansenist propositions of Quesnel, but the few that deal with the reading of the Bible and its role in Catholic life are still surprising and puzzling. Yet they are part of the post-Tridentine heritage, which came to an end only in the last half of the twentieth century, especially under the influence of the Second Vatican Council.

The preconciliar Catholic Church in the twentieth century was a deeply eucharistic Church, in which most of the faithful had no idea of what the "Word of God" was all about. Catholic life was centered then on the Mass, and Catholics lived by the words of the Church:

occasional encyclicals of the Holy Father, pastoral instructions of their diocesan bishops, and the catechism in its various forms taught by priests and religious. Readings from the written Word of God or the Bible were used in the Mass, but that was celebrated usually in Latin, and the readings were not always used for the topic of the sermon. The result was that many Catholics at that time lived abiblical or nonbiblical lives. All that changed with what happened at the Second Vatican Council, convoked by the charismatic Pope John XXIII.

Before I turn to the teaching and the effect of the Second Vatican Council itself, I must deal with the antecedents of the Council, in order to put its teaching about Scripture in a proper perspective. My further remarks, then, will be made under three headings: (1) the antecedents of the Second Vatican Council in the area of biblical studies; (2) the teaching of Vatican II on Scripture; and (3) the impact of that teaching on the life of the Church.

1. The Antecedents of the Second Vatican Council in the Area of Biblical Studies

I have always maintained that there never would have been a Second Vatican Council, if it were not for the 1943 encyclical of Pope Pius XII, *Divino afflante Spiritu*, "On the Promotion of Biblical Studies." We have all heard of that encyclical, but not many of us realize its importance. It was a "sleeper," because its effects did not immediately see fruition, and it took a while for Catholic people to become aware of what it was all about. The main reason for the delayed reaction to this encyclical was that it was issued in 1943, during the Second World War, when the minds of most people in the countries involved in that war were preoccupied with things other than the interpretation of the Bible. With the end of World War II, there emerged in Europe what was called *la nouvelle théologie* (especially in the 1950s). It was heavily dependent on a new way of reading, studying, and interpreting Scripture, in effect on the way that Pope Pius XII had recommended. This new theology and the encyclical of Pope Pius XII thus provided the background and stimulus for the Council.

Before I say more about the importance of that encyclical, I must recall two other factors, which were among the antecedents, not only of

Pius XII's encyclical, but of the Second Vatican Council itself. The first of these factors was the encyclical of Pope Leo XIII, *Providentissimus Deus*, "On the Study of Scripture," issued on 18 November 1893.[4] *Divino afflante Spiritu* of Pope Pius XII was composed to celebrate the fiftieth anniversary of Leo XIII's letter. Toward the end of the nineteenth century, Léo XIII had to cope with the effects of the so-called Enlightenment and its radical approach to life and the critical interpretation of ancient documents, such as the Bible, as it sought to be rid of dogma, revelation, or anything supernatural.

Leo XIII also recognized the tremendous historical, archaeological, and scientific discoveries of the nineteenth century, which profoundly affected the interpretation of the Bible, e.g., the decipherment of the Rosetta Stone, which revealed the treasures of the literature of the Egyptians, neighbors of ancient Israel to the west, and that of the Bisitun Stone, which revealed the literature of the Assyrians and Babylonians, neighbors of Israel to the east.[5] Thus, for the first time the biblical writings of the OT could be read in the ancient context in which they had been composed. The result of such discoveries made it clear that the Bible did not drop from heaven, and that it could no longer be interpreted without serious consideration of the similar and kindred literary forms found in this newly discovered Egyptian and Assyrian/Babylonian literature.

Because of the critical spirit of the Enlightenment, German historicism, the *Babel-Bibel* disputes, and because of the new discoveries and the scientific advances in biology and evolution, a radically rationalist way of thinking and interpreting emerged, which Leo XIII sought to cope with in his encyclical *Providentissimus Deus*. All of this contributed to the Modernism that marked the end of the nineteenth and the beginning of the twentieth century in the Catholic Church.

The second factor that led up to *Divino afflante Spiritu* was the establishment of the Pontifical Biblical Commission by Pope Leo XIII in 1902 with his Apostolic Letter *Vigilantiae studiique*.[6] It was an effort to further biblical scholarship and safeguard the authority of Scripture against attacks of exaggerated criticism. The first word of that Letter, *Vigilantiae*, however, set the tone for the Commission's work, because it had the task of a watchdog, or of vigilantes. Among other things, it had to answer questions posed to it on biblical matters; its *responsa* dealt with such matters as the Mosaic authorship of the Pentateuch

(1906), the authenticity and historicity of the Johannine Gospel (1907), the historicity of Genesis 1–3 (1909). Although such *responsa* were never meant to be infallible, Pope Pius X later required of Catholics the same submission to them as to similar papally approved decrees of other Roman congregations. The result was that the Commission's *responsa* cast a dark cloud of fear and reactionary conservatism over Catholic clergy and biblical scholars in the first half of the twentieth century. Although Leo XIII acted rightly in both issuing his encyclical of 1893 and establishing the Biblical Commission in 1902, the effects of his actions, certainly unintended, were not always in the best interests of Catholic study of the Bible or of Catholic life in general.

These two factors, the encyclical of Leo XIII and the work of the Biblical Commission in the early years of the twentieth century, provided the background for the 1943 encyclical of Pope Pius XII. Issued on the feast of St. Jerome (30 September) in 1943, it was a liberating force, because, though he never named the method, Pius XII advocated the proper use of the historical-critical method of interpreting the Bible in order to ascertain the literal sense of the biblical text. In its first part, Pius XII recalled the historical background of biblical studies in the Church (the encyclical of Leo XIII, various decisions of Popes Pius X and XI, the founding of the Ecole Biblique in Jerusalem [1890], the institution of the Biblical Commission). In the second part, he built on the directives of Leo XIII, recalled the archaeological and historical discoveries, and stressed the need of recourse to the original languages of the Bible, from which all future vernacular translations for use in the Church henceforth were to be made. Furthermore, he insisted on the interpretation of the Bible according to its literal sense, "that the mind of the author may be made abundantly clear." This insistence on the literal sense did not commit Catholic interpreters to any fundamentalistic literalism, but it meant that the real, religious meaning of the written Word of God had to be ascertained. Pius XII also spoke of the "spiritual sense" of Scripture, but he used that term only in its traditional meaning, i.e., the christological sense of the OT. Besides the literal sense, the interpreter must explain this spiritual sense, "provided it is clearly intended by God." However, the "allegorical" sense, which was used often by patristic interpreters and even recommended by Leo XIII, was not mentioned by Pius XII. He admitted, however, that "figurative senses" of Scripture might be useful in preaching, but he cautioned that such senses are "extrinsic to it and accidental" and "especially in these days, not free from danger." Moreover, Pius XII clarified that "there are but few texts whose sense has been defined by the teaching authority of the Church," and fewer still "about which the teaching of the Holy Fathers is unanimous." The encyclical's primary emphasis fell on the interpretation of the Bible according to its "literary forms," espousing an idea that Pope Benedict XV had rejected.

In thus setting forth guidelines for interpreting Scripture, Pius XII advocated the proper use of the mode of interpretation that had been utilized for decades by both Protestant and Jewish interpreters, the so-called historical-critical method of interpretation.[7] As a result, the interpretation of the Bible by Catholic scholars in the second half of the twentieth century began to rival that of their Protestant and Jewish peers. It also invigorated the study of Catholic theology, for it provided it with a solid biblical basis. This change in the mode of Catholic interpretation of the Bible was noted above all at the Second Vatican Council by the Protestant observers, who gradually realized that Catholics were now venerating and interpreting Scripture the way that they had been. This change led not only to the Second Vatican Council, but also in due course to the ecumenical openness of the Catholic Church to other Christian ecclesial communities.

2. The Teaching of Vatican II on Scripture

Although many documents of the Second Vatican Council made use of Scripture in the course of their composition, the direct teaching of the Council on Scripture is found in the six chapters of the Dogmatic Constitution on Divine Revelation (*Dei Verbum*, "The Word of God").[8] After a short prologue, the Constitution defines revelation as the way God makes known himself and his will through creation and especially through his son Jesus Christ for the salvation of mankind: "We proclaim to you the eternal life that was with the Father and was made visible to us…; for our fellowship is with the Father and with his Son, Jesus Christ" (1 John 1:2–3). Revelation is, then, not simply a communication of knowledge but a dynamic process by which the divine persons invite human beings to enter into a relation of fellowship (chap. 1).[9] It further teaches how that self-revelation of God is transmitted to all generations through the gospel of Christ preached by the apostles and their successors with the help of the Holy Spirit and is expressed in Tradition and Scripture, a single deposit of the Word of God. It thus emphasizes the inseparability of Scripture and Tradition and avoids saying that there are any revealed truths transmitted solely by Tradition (chap. 2). The Constitution likewise affirms the inspiration of Scripture, teaching that it has God as its author, who speaks through human agents and in human fashion so that one must attend to the literary forms used and to the unity of Scripture in order to ascertain the intention of the inspired writers and to realize that the sacred books teach firmly, faithfully, and without error the truth that God wanted to be recorded for the sake of our salvation (chap. 3). The Constitution then describes the OT as the preparation for the salvation of all humanity in the choice of a people to whom divine promises were entrusted gradually and as a preparation for the coming of Christ, stressing that these OT books have meaning even for Christians (chap. 4). In chap. 5, the Constitution shows how the Word of God, which is God's power for the salvation of believers, is set forth in the writings of the NT, preeminently in the four Gospels of apostolic origin, but also in other writings, all of which have to be understood properly. Finally, in chap. 6, the Constitution sets forth how Scripture plays a role in the life of the Church, by being, along with Tradition, the supreme rule of faith, because in it our heavenly Father speaks to and meets his children; for this reason easy access to Scripture should be available to the Christian faithful in accurate vernacular translations.

What I have just stated is a very brief résumé of the six chapters of this Dogmatic Constitution of the Second Vatican Council. Now I should like to select four particular points that make this conciliar document so important and that have contributed in a distinctive way to the role that Scripture has been playing in the Catholic Church in the last forty some years.

First, in chap. 3 the Constitution stresses the venerable and traditional teaching about the inspiration of Scripture, echoing the doctrine of the Council of Trent and the First Vatican Council, but it relates to that traditional teaching an important assertion about inerrancy. To explain this adequately, I must make a preliminary point about inspiration and revelation, because some Christians fail to distinguish them properly. Inspiration is not a charism that makes the writing a revelation. The Constitution had already defined revelation in chap. 1 as the self-manifestation of a personal God and the making known of the mystery of his will for the salvation of humanity. Inspiration is rather the charism by which human beings were moved by God (or by the Spirit of God) to record aspects or details of that divine revelation. The two ideas are not the same, or even coterminous. It is conceivable that a whole biblical book is inspired, from the first word to the last, and yet not contain revelation. Many of the aphorisms or maxims in Ecclesiastes or in the Book of Proverbs are nuggets of human wisdom, inspired indeed, but saying nothing about the self-revealing God, his will, or his designs for human salvation. For instance, Prov 21:9 reads, "It is better to live in a corner of the housetop than in a house shared with a contentious wife"; that is repeated in 25:24. Such a saying passes on inspired wisdom, but it is not revelation; it tells us nothing about God or his will.

When one comes to inerrancy, it has to be understood as a consequence of inspiration, but one that is not coterminous with it. It is restricted to inspired statements in the Bible, and not to its questions, exclamations, or prayers. For the Constitution plainly states, "Since everything asserted by the inspired authors or sacred writers should be regarded as asserted by the Holy Spirit, it follows that we must acknowledge the Books of Scripture as teaching firmly, faithfully, and without error the truth that God wished to be recorded in the sacred writings for the sake of our salvation" (§11).[10] Especially noteworthy are two things: the verb "asserted," which is used twice, and the last phrase, "recorded…for the sake of our salvation." In other words, inerrancy is the quality of all assertions in the Bible that pertain to human salvation. That important phrase saves Catholic interpreters from crass fundamentalism, because it means that the charism of inerrancy does not necessarily grace every statement made with a past tense verb as if it were historically true. For this reason, the Constitution continues in §12 with a discussion about the relation of biblical truth to "literary forms": "Truth is differently presented and expressed in various types of historical writings, in prophetic or poetic texts, or in other modes of speech. Furthermore, the interpreter must search for what meaning the sacred writer, in his own historical situation and in accordance with the condition of his time and culture, intended to express and did in fact express with the help of literary forms that were in use during that time." In this regard, the Constitution was reiterating merely what Pius XII had said less directly in *Divino afflante Spiritu* §§20–21.[11]

Second, the Constitution stresses that Tradition and Sacred Scripture flow "from the same divine wellspring, in a certain way come together into a single current, and tend to the same end," because they "form a single deposit of the Word of God, which is entrusted to the Church" (§10), and which is transmitted by its teaching, life, and worship. This idea is noteworthy, because, even though the Council Fathers knew that some theologians had regarded Scripture and Tradition as two separate fonts or sources of revelation and did not want to condemn that view, they resolutely stated their own position about the single deposit of the Word of God.

The Constitution continues, however, with a still more important notion:

> The task of authentically interpreting the Word of God, whether in its written form or in the form of tradition, has been entrusted to the Teaching Office of the Church, whose authority is exercised in the name of Jesus Christ. Indeed, this Teaching Office is not above the Word of God but serves it by teaching only what has been handed on. At the divine command and with the help of the Holy Spirit, the Teaching Office listens to the Word of God devoutly, guards it with dedication, and faithfully explains it. All that it proposes for belief as divinely revealed is drawn from this single deposit of faith. (§10)[12]

This relation of the Teaching Office *(magisterium)* to the Word of God is a novel notion, never before enunciated in the Church's teaching about Scripture. Note, however, the emphasis: the Teaching Office "is not above the Word of God but serves it by teaching only what has been handed on." It does not say that the Teaching Office is not above the *written* Word of God or Scripture. Yet that meaning of "the Word of God" is not excluded, because in the preceding sentence "the Word of God" is qualified, "whether in its written form or in the form of tradition." What the Constitution was trying to offset was the criticism sometimes heard that for Catholics the ultimate norm of belief is the magisterium. The careful formulation of §10 of *Dei Verbum* sought to correct such a view.

Third, a striking paragraph in the Constitution is found in chap. 5, when the Gospels of the NT are discussed. I am referring to §19, which I shall quote in full:

> Holy Mother Church has firmly and constantly held and continues to hold that the four Gospels just named, whose historicity the Church affirms without hesitation, faithfully hand on what Jesus, the Son of God, while he lived among men and women, actually did and taught for their eternal salvation, until the day when he was taken up (cf. Acts 1:1–2). For, after the ascension of the Lord, the apostles handed on to their hearers what Jesus had said and done, and they did this with that fuller understanding they now enjoyed, having been instructed by the glorious events of Christ and taught by the light of the Spirit of truth. In composing the four Gospels, the sacred writers selected certain of the many traditions that had been handed on either orally or already in written form; others they summarized or explicated with an eye to the situation of the churches. Moreover, they retained the form and style of proclamation but always in such a fashion that they related to us an honest and true account of Jesus. For their intention in writing was that, either from their own memory and recollections or from the testimony of those "who from the beginning were eyewitnesses and ministers of the Word" we might know "the truth" concerning the things about which we have been instructed (cf. Luke 1:2–4).[13]

The paragraph begins with "Holy Mother Church," a phrase that is derived from the title of a document published by the Biblical Commission, which by the time of the Second Vatican Council had long since changed its image. It was no longer the watchdog commission of old, because after Pius XII's encyclical of 1943 it had begun to issue positive teachings of considerable value. In 1964, during the Council itself, the Commission composed a remarkable text,

"Instruction on the Historical Truth of the Gospels," the opening words of which are *Sancta Mater Ecclesia*.[14] It was remarkable, because it did not simply reiterate the historicity of the four Gospels, but gave a very nuanced interpretation of the gospel tradition, showing that anyone who interpreted the Gospels had to reckon with the three stages of their formation. It turned out that the most important word in the title was not the adjective *historica*, which might have been one's initial expectation, but the preposition *de*, "about, on." The Constitution even bears a footnote (n. 35) that refers to the Biblical Commission's Instruction. (For further details about this Instruction, see chapter 3 below, where the text is given in an English translation and commented on.)

The Dogmatic Constitution on Divine Revelation also acknowledges that Scripture has to be the soul of theology. In its final chapter, on the role that Scripture has to play in the life of the Church, the Constitution recognizes that both Scripture and Tradition are the "permanent foundation" of sacred theology: "The Sacred Scriptures contain the Word of God, and, because they are inspired, they are truly the Word of God. Therefore, let the study of the sacred page be, as it were, the soul of Sacred Theology" (§24).[15] The Second Vatican Council referred to the same idea in its Decree on Priestly Formation, *Optatam totius* §16.[16] In saying that, the Council Fathers were echoing what Pope Leo XIII had written in *Providentissimus Deus*, "It is most desirable and necessary that the use of the same sacred Scripture should influence the discipline of theology and be, as it were, its soul" *(eiusque proprie sit anima)*.[17] Such a role of Scripture is, of course, rightly taken for granted today, but it was not always so.[18]

Prior to the Second World War (and so, prior to Pope Pius XII's encyclical), theologians often used Scripture merely as a sourcebook for proof texts to support theses spun out almost independently of the Bible. No less a theologian than Karl Rahner once sought to correct that and to establish a mutual dialogue between Catholic exegetes and dogmatic theologians. In an article entitled "Exegese und Dogmatik," Rahner discussed the role of both exegetes and theologians, addressing the former with the formal second plural German pronoun "Ihr," but using the familiar "Du," when he addressed his colleagues, fellow dogmatic theologians.[19] To the exegetes he said, You must remember that you too "are Catholic theologians," that you must pay attention to "the Catholic principles governing the relationship between exegesis and dogmatic theology," that you must learn to build a bridge from your investigations and interpretations to the rest of theology, and that you should have "a more exact knowledge of scholastic theology." Rahner, however, chided his colleagues:

> You know less about exegesis than you should. As a dogmatic theologian you rightly claim to be allowed to engage in the work of exegesis and biblical theology in your own right, and not just to accept the results of the exegetical work of the specialist....But then you must perform the work of exegesis in the way it has to be done today and not in the way you used to do it in the good old days....Your exegesis in dogmatic theology must be convincing also to the specialist in exegesis."[20]

Rahner wrote those words the year before the Second Vatican Council opened, but he was already aware of the idea that Scripture had to be the soul of theology.

3. The Impact of the Council's Teaching on the Life of the Church

Dei Verbum ends with chap. 6 discussing the role of Sacred Scripture in the life of the Church. The chapter begins by asserting that "the Church has always venerated the Divine Scriptures just as she venerates the Body of the Lord, never ceasing to offer to the faithful, especially in the sacred liturgy, the bread of life, received from the one table of God's Word and Christ's Body" (§21). Here "the bread of life" is given a double connotation, simultaneous sustenance from the Word and the Sacrament. In asserting that, the Council Fathers were stressing once again what had been taught in the Constitution on the Liturgy, viz., that the liturgy of the Word was not just a preliminary part of the Catholic Mass, something that could really be dispensed with, but of basically equal value with the liturgy of the Eucharist, because the Church, as the body of Christ, is also the community of the Logos, and is fed by both his word and his flesh and blood.

Vatican II, for that reason, insisted that "easy access to the Sacred Scriptures should be available to the Christian faithful," which means that "the Church with motherly concern sees to it that suitable and accurate translations are made into various languages, especially from the original texts of the sacred Books" (§22). In this, the Council Fathers were again echoing the instruction of Pope Pius XII. They went further, however, in saying, "If it should happen, provided the opportunity arises and the authorities of the Church agree, that these translations are also produced in cooperation with the separated brethren, then all Christians will be able to use them" (§22). We have seen that happen in the use of the *Revised Standard Version* of the Bible in the English-speaking countries of the world.

Even though the Constitution had earlier insisted on Scripture as the written Word of God, it now stresses that, along with the Tradition that has grown out of it, as the Church has been living through the centuries, Scripture remains the supreme rule of faith. Karl Rahner explained the relation of Scripture and Tradition by adopting a famous Lutheran distinction, according to which Scripture is the *norma normans non normata* and Tradition is the *norma normata.* That is, Scripture is the norm that norms faith and all else in the Church, but is itself not normed, whereas Tradition is a norm of faith and life, but it is normed (by Scripture).[21] The reason for Rahner's adoption of this explanation was that for him, Tradition is nothing more than "a legitimate unfolding of the biblical data."[22] So understood, it is easy to comprehend how the twosome can be called a single deposit and the supreme rule of faith.

Again, even though the Constitution stresses that "the interpreter of Sacred Scripture…should carefully search out what the sacred writers truly intended to express and what God thought well to manifest by their words" (§12), it emphasizes also the need for all to realize that "in the sacred Books, the Father who is in heaven comes lovingly to meet his children and speaks with them; so great is the force and power of God's Word that it remains the sustaining life-force of the Church, the strength of faith for her children, the nourishment for the soul, and the pure and lasting source of spiritual life" (§21). For the revealing God still addresses Christians of the twenty-first century as he did during the millennium in which the two Testaments originally came into being, and precisely through the same words (accurately translated).

What is behind these conciliar statements is the distinction often applied to Scripture between *what it meant* to the sacred author and *what it means* to Christians today. The Word of God encapsulated in the words of the ancient human author revealed to him thoughts and words that were important not only to him and the ancient people for whom he recorded them, but also for believers throughout the ages who have found and still find inspiration for their lives in both the OT and the NT. God spoke through the Scriptures to his people of old, the contemporaries of the sacred writers; but he also speaks through the same inspired words to his people of today. Consequently, then, there must be a homogeneity between what it meant and what it means. What it means cannot be so diverse or different from what it meant, because then God's Word as revelation would not continue to be passed on.

It is in terms of this problem that one has to mention another document of the Biblical Commission, which appeared almost thirty years after the close of the Second Vatican Council, *The Interpretation of the Bible in the Church*, issued in 1993.[23] It is a remarkable document, which has been highly praised by Catholic, Jewish, and Protestant scholars. It builds on the teaching of Vatican II, taking most of the Council's teaching for granted, but in one respect it goes significantly beyond the Council. That has to do with what the Commission calls "actualization" of the written Word of God. It makes use of a French word, *actualisation*, which basically means "modernization" or "making present." Technically, it denotes the actualization of the literal sense of the ancient human authors' inspired words, ascertained by the historical-critical method of interpretation. Those words are reread in the light of new circumstances and applied to the contemporary situation of God's people; their message is expressed in language adapted to the present time. The Commission reckoned with the wealth of meaning of the biblical text, which gives it a value for all times and cultures. Though the biblical text is of lasting value, it sometimes is time-conditioned in its expression. There are, moreover, a dynamic unity and a complex relationship between the two Testaments, which must be acknowledged.[24]

Such actualization often involves what is called in French *relecture*, a rereading of the ancient text in the light of present-day events.[25] The model for such *relecture* is found in the Bible itself, when words, phrases, or themes of older written texts are used in new circumstances that add new meaning to the original sense, which was open to it. For instance, motifs from the Exodus are taken up in Deutero-Isaiah to give consolation to the people of Israel returning from the Babylonian Captivity (e.g., the motifs of Exod 15:1–8, the Song of Moses, are so used in Isa 42:10–13, which calls on all to praise God as the victorious warrior; or those of Exodus 14—15, the passage through the Reed Sea, are so used in Isa 43:16–17; 41:17–20); or when motifs from the plagues of Egypt and deliverance from Egypt are taken up in Wisdom 11—19. The Commission, however, also cautions that none of these broadening aspects can be invoked to "attribute to a biblical text whatever meaning we like, interpreting it in a wholly subjective way," because that would be to introduce "alien meanings" into the text and to disrupt the homogeneity between what it meant and what it means.

Toward the end of chap. 6, *Dei Verbum* addresses priests and bishops about their obligations:

> Therefore all clerics, especially priests of Christ and others who are officially engaged as deacons and catechists in the ministry of the Word, must hold fast to the Scriptures through diligent spiritual reading and careful study. This obligation must be fulfilled lest any of them become "an empty preacher of the Divine Word outwardly, who is not a listener inwardly,"[26] when they ought to be sharing with all the faithful committed to their care the abundant riches of the Divine Word, especially in the sacred liturgy. The sacred Synod strongly and explicitly urges all the Christian faithful, as well, and especially religious, to learn by frequent reading of the Divine Scriptures "the supreme good of knowing Jesus Christ" (Phil 3:8), "For ignorance of the Scriptures is ignorance of Christ" [quoting St. Jerome[27]]. (§25)

The final paragraph of *Dei Verbum* is fittingly quoted:

> In this way, therefore, let "the Word of God speed forward and be glorified" (2 Thess 3:1), and let the treasure of revelation entrusted to the Church fill human hearts ever more and more. Just as from constant participation in the

eucharistic mystery the life of the Church draws strength, so we may hope for a new surge of spiritual vitality from a greater veneration of the Word of God, which "stands forever" (Isa 40:8; cf. 1 Pet 1:23–25). (§26)

In conclusion, then, one can see readily how far the Catholic Church has come from the days of Pope Clement XI, whose Constitution *Unigenitus Dei Filius* condemned the proposition of Pasquier Quesnel that "the reading of Sacred Scripture is for everybody." The teaching of the Second Vatican Council about Scripture and its role in the life of the Church sanctioned, confirmed, and at times extended the efforts of two great Popes of the nineteenth and twentieth centuries who strove to promote the proper veneration and study of the Bible in order to enhance the spiritual lives of the Catholic faithful. *Dei Verbum* was joined at the Second Vatican Council with another important document, *Sacrosanctum Concilium* on the Divine Liturgy, and the two of them have made a tremendous difference in the life of the Catholic Church. If the Church in the preconciliar days was deeply eucharistic in its life, the ecumenical council added a new factor in *Dei Verbum*. Today we are all aware how much we have profited from the renewed biblical source of our Catholic lives, which received a climactic impulse in the teaching of the Second Vatican Council.

2

A ROMAN SCRIPTURE CONTROVERSY

As an example of the way that the interpretation of Scripture fared in pre–Vatican II days, one can recall the controversy that surrounded it in the city of Rome itself about 1960. For it has been the lot of dedicated Scripture scholars to be the target of well-meaning critics who fail to comprehend their intentions and claim that their work undermines Christian faith. This, however, is not a phenomenon restricted to the twentieth century, as an incident in the life of St. Jerome shows. The incident is recounted here to serve as a background for a similar event in Rome prior to the Second Vatican Council.

Between the years A.D. 389 and 392, Jerome translated anew the OT prophets into Latin from the *hebraica veritas* (Hebrew truth), as he was wont to refer to the original Hebrew text. When he reached the fourth chapter of the Book of Jonah, where the prophet in distress of soul and wishing to die goes out of the city of Nineveh and sits down in a hut that he had made for himself, Jerome translated v. 6 as follows: *Et praeparavit Dominus Deus hederam et ascendit super caput Ionae ut esset umbra super caput eius et protegeret eum* (The Lord God prepared ivy, and it grew up over Jonah's head, that it might be a shade over his head and protect him).

The bishop of an African town sanctioned the reading of Jerome's new translation in his churches. When the people heard the familiar passage with the new word *hedera* (ivy) instead of *cucurbita* (gourd) of older Latin translations based on the Septuagint, such a tumult ensued that the bishop had to consult some Jews, who told him that *cucurbita* was the sense of the Hebrew.[1]

In A.D. 403, Augustine, who had already been a bishop for about eight years, wrote to Jerome about this incident and protested against the innovation, *hedera* instead of *cucurbita*, because of the effect that it had on the African bishop's flock. He concluded by suggesting that possibly Jerome was not always right: "And so it seems also to us that you too at times could have erred in some respects."[2] Jerome replied by

17

explaining that, though the Septuagint had "gourd," other Greek translators including Aquila had used "ivy," and that the Hebrew word actually designated a plant called by the Syrians of his day *ciceion*.[3] "If I had wanted merely to transcribe *ciceion*, no one would have understood me; if I put down 'gourd,' I would be saying what is not in the Hebrew; so I put 'ivy' to agree with other translators."[4] Augustine answered in A.D. 405 that he still preferred *cucurbita*, the meaning of the word in the Septuagint. Since he regarded the Septuagint as inspired, he begged Jerome for a good translation of it.[5] He also informed the exegete of Bethlehem, who was more interested in the *hebraica veritas*, "I do not wish your translation from the Hebrew to be read in the churches, for fear of upsetting the flock of Christ with great scandal, by publishing something new, something seemingly contrary to the authority of the Septuagint, which version their ears and hearts are accustomed to hear, and which was accepted even by the apostles."[6]

The mentality of Augustine displayed in this incident is somewhat akin to that which modern Scripture scholars meet in their attempts to set forth the meaning of certain biblical passages. In Jerome's day, it was a question of translation; today it is a question of interpretation; but the fear is the same: *ne...tamquam novum aliquid proferentes magno scandalo perturbemus plebes Christi* (for fear of upsetting the flock of Christ with great scandal by publishing something new). When we read Jonah 4:6 today in the Vulgate, none of us suspects the controversy that it occasioned. Yet Jerome's translation *hedera* has remained for centuries, while Augustine's story of the African bishop is recalled as an interesting incident — if not a fable — by the biographers of the learned, irascible, impatient, but saintly Eusebius Hieronymus.

The reaction to modern Catholic biblical scholars has been at times unfortunately quite similar to that of Augustine, a fear that the biblical innovation will upset something. The manifestation of such a reaction took place in Rome in the early 1960s. The nature of it and its consequences have been forgotten already, but they were such that it is important to attempt to reconstruct the happenings, insofar as they can be controlled, because they could be repeated in areas far from Rome, where the issue also could become clouded.

I

Luis Alonso Schökel, S.J., a young Spanish professor of the OT at the Pontifical Biblical Institute in Rome, wrote an article in 1960 entitled, "Where Is Catholic Exegesis Headed?"[7] In twelve pages, he sought to answer the question that he put to himself in the title. Here is a résumé of his article:

> "Where is Catholic exegesis headed?" This question is often asked. It reveals a certain friendly preoccupation, and it should be answered by the exegete with simplicity and clarity. To answer the question, it is well to consider the path along which Catholic exegesis has been proceeding in the period between two pronouncements of Pope Pius XII, *Divino afflante Spiritu* (1943) and his message to the Congrès International Catholique des Sciences Bibliques held at the time of the Brussels Fair (1958). In the future, it will certainly follow this path.
>
> Such an apparently simple way of answering the question is in reality complicated. For during that period there took place a remarkable change of direction in biblical studies, when they are compared with the preceding fifty years — not to mention previous centuries. Consequently, one must go back to the beginning of the twentieth century to put the question in its proper light.
>
> The first part of the article cites examples of the new direction that had been adopted in various areas of biblical studies. In each case, a striking contrast is seen, when one compares statements in the writings of Catholic scholars of the beginning of the century, such as L. Murillo, L. Fonck, and L. Billot, with statements of Pius XII in *Divino afflante Spiritu* and *Humani generis* apropos of the same subject. Billot treated with ironic disdain the knowledge of ambient cultures and languages of the ancient Near East, whereas Pius XII stressed that "all these advantages which…our age has acquired are, as it were, an invitation and inducement to interpreters of sacred literature to make diligent use of this light, so abundantly given, to penetrate more deeply,

19

explain more clearly, and expound more lucidly the divine oracles"[8] Whereas Billot had branded literary genres as "genera vanitatis" and concluded that the Bible's genre was "singulare, transcendens, nullam cum aliis comparationem ferens" (unique, transcendent, and bearing no comparison with others), Pius XII imposed on Catholic interpreters the obligation of studying the genres used in Scripture. Murillo, who rejected the possibility of popular traditions in Genesis 1–11, held out for their "perfectly historical character." Yet while it is obvious that both Pius XII and Murillo agree on the fundamental truth of biblical inerrancy, the Pope frankly admitted in those chapters a mode of speaking adapted to the mentality of a people but little cultured, which gives a popular description of the origin of the human race and the Chosen People. Fonck had argued that the Bible presents us with a series of historical books (as tradition attests); but history narrates facts in direct judgments. Hence the Bible enjoys a total historicity infallibly narrated; any liberty taken by the hagiographer would be irreconcilable with inspiration. The encyclicals of Pius XII, however, frankly admit that the historical narratives are not to be judged by modern critical methods or even by those of the ancient Greeks and Romans, although they do belong to a genre of history that is to be studied and determined by the exegete. Apropos of patristic interpretations, Murillo maintained that a unanimous consent of the Fathers resulted in a *de fide* interpretation, no matter what the subject is (e.g., that Moses wrote the Pentateuch). Pius XII, however, pointed out clearly that there are few texts about which the teaching of the Fathers is unanimous[9] and that "especially in matters pertaining to history" the commentators of past ages lacked almost all the information that was needed for their clear exposition. Finally, Fonck was most skeptical of new methods and solutions and found in them nothing solid, whereas *Divino afflante Spiritu* openly admitted that, if new problems have arisen, new methods and tools have also been discovered that aid in their solution. These comparisons are not intended as an accusation of scholars of yesterday, who were *bene meriti*, but only as concrete evidence of a change of direction in the path followed by Catholic interpreters.

The second part of the article makes three observations that are necessary to fill out the picture. First, the change of direction did not come about like an unforeseen earthquake, for *Divino afflante Spiritu* merely crystallized and canonized the results of private study carried on by many interpreters. Today's positions are often the results of the work of scholars well before 1943. For instance, a century ago Catholic and Protestant commentators agreed in considering Solomon the author of Qoheleth. After Delitzsch denied the Solomonic authorship of that book in 1875, he was followed by the Catholics A. Condamin, S.J., in 1900 and E. Podechard in 1913. Though about 1920 that was a suspect opinion in some Catholic circles, A. Vaccari, another professor at the Biblical Institute, espoused it in 1930. Today, even the most conservative Catholic scholars deny the Solomonic authorship of Qoheleth. There is thus a certain *continuity* with what preceded 1943. Second, many points established and defended by older exegetes are still maintained, such as inerrancy and the exclusion of "historical appearances" and of other radical positions. Third, it should be remembered that before 1943, along with a "strict" school of conservative interpreters, there also existed a broadminded group. In some cases, certain individuals of the latter group erred, and their errors were rejected both by the Church's authority and by the progress of biblical studies itself (e.g., "historical appearances," defended by P. F. de Hummelauer; certain infelicitous formulations of P. M.-J. Lagrange). Others of this school, however, legitimately counterbalanced the "strict" school, and the continuity between the directives of Pius XII and the positions of the former is evident. Hence, that present-day Catholic exegesis follows that of fifty years ago in many points does not surprise anyone; but that it is following a new path in other matters should not surprise anyone who has followed the encyclicals. Thus an answer is given, in part at least, to the initial question.

The third part of the article attempts to explain where Catholic exegesis has been heading since 1943. When Pius XII published his encyclical, he was aware that he was opening a door to innovations in exegesis that might excite conservative minds; for he dedicated a paragraph of the encyclical to the defense of the liberty of those who would work seriously in the area of exegesis.[10] It was an act of confidence on the part of Pius XII immediately in Catholic interpreters and indirectly in the Holy Spirit who guides the Church. But have not the interpreters failed the Pope? Have they not strayed from the path assigned to them? In fact, the encyclical of 1950, *Humani generis*, bemoans just such deviations.[11] It should be noted, however, that among the errors proscribed there are some more "theological" than "exegetical," referring not to the interpretation of individual texts, but to principles of inspiration and hermeneutics (e.g., the sense of the formula "God Author of Scripture," inerrancy, relation of Scripture to the magisterium, "spiritual" interpretation). Historicity was treated in another paragraph, in which too lax an interpretation of the letter sent to Cardinal Suhard of Paris was deplored.[12] But is not this danger still with us? For, though Pius XII had accorded liberty of scientific investigation to interpreters, he did so with certain limits and cautions (e.g., the analogy of faith, a prudence based on solid and honest scientific research). To pass judgment on the historicity of a biblical passage without sufficient evidence is a dangerous procedure, for it can compromise data important for the history of salvation and create serious doubts and trouble. Thus, whoever would affirm the entire historicity of the Book of Judith puts the reader in serious difficulties from the very first verses; whoever would deny all historicity to Matthew 16 would create serious difficulties for the primacy of Peter. The present crisis stems from some exegetes who treat the problem of historicity with insufficiently grounded arguments and from popularizers who delight in launching immature and

22

undigested results of research among the general public. The limits of prudence and charity, however, must be respected both in scientific research and in popularization; in fact, charity makes demands that transcend the liberty or research or exposition. Three bishops at the Brussels Congress complained of the lack of competence and prudence displayed by popularizers; the Bishop of Namur, in particular, stressed that the discussion of complex and delicate biblical questions should be left to professional exegetes, qualified to handle them. The statements of these bishops, together with *Humani generis*, indicate that there have been errors and abuses of the liberty of investigation. There is, however, no need to point the finger at individuals or regions; a priori, one can say that the number of errors will be greater there where the popularization has been more intense. The Bishop of Namur emphasized: "We know that [Catholic exegetes] apply themselves to their work with good will, with fervor and even with enthusiasm, and we think they measure up in general very well to the Church's confidence in them. They err sometimes?...But are we to believe that those who never err are always *eo ipso* the best collaborators of the hierarchy?... They [the exegetes] offer the hierarchy their good will, their labors, and the results of their research. And we can say that the hierarchy on its side looks for this collaboration with confidence and welcomes it with gratitude" (*Sacra pagina* 1.78–79).

In conclusion, Catholic exegesis is proceeding along the path traced for it by Pius XII in *Divino afflante Spiritu*, which was at once a beacon and a stimulus. Questions that have been resolved by now have been incorporated calmly into biblical science; new problems continue to arise and engage the exegetes. Certainly, errors and deviations have occurred. This is because the exegetes, though guided in their research by the light of revelation and aided by the methods of their science, are not endowed with infallibility. The danger of deviation from the path is always present, but the guidance of the magisterium and serious scientific work are sufficient to cope with it. This was the burden of the address of Pope John XXIII to the Pontifical Biblical Institute on the occasion of its jubilee, and also of Pius XII to the Catholic exegetes gathered at Brussels from many lands — the successors of the "strict" school in many principles, the successors of the "broadminded" school in many questions of method.

It is recognized that the article of Alonso Schökel, calmly considered, aimed at bringing together within a few pages many things that have been known and accepted in Catholic theological and exegetical circles for a long time. It had the merit of putting the question of modern biblical studies in a perspective that had been badly needed. The only way to explain the "new direction" has been to sketch the matrix in which it had its origin. This Alonso Schökel did, and in general he achieved it with laudable success, despite a few oversimplifications that a brief article of twelve pages might inevitably contain. The article was an effort of a competent biblical interpreter who knew whereof he was speaking.

II

The article, however, was not accorded a welcome reception in all quarters. In particular, Msgr. Antonino Romeo, a domestic prelate from Reggio Calabria, professor of Scripture at the Lateran University in Rome, published a seventy-page article entitled "The Encyclical 'Divino afflante Spiritu' and the 'New Opinions,'"[13] the main part of which offers a severe criticism of Alonso Schökel's article. The reader of Romeo's criticism soon realizes that it was motivated by something more than the explanations of Alonso Schökel, which were only part of the "New Opinions." What the real motivation was remains obscure.[14] However, such severe criticism, coming from a person like Msgr. Romeo in such a significant position, raised the question: Was this an official view that was being voiced? Was this a reaction of Roman congregations to the "new direction" in biblical studies, of which Alonso Schökel had written? Was this the start of a political move of the Lateran University against the Biblical Institute?

24

The burden of Romeo's article is a denial that the encyclical *Divino afflante Spiritu* is responsible for any new direction in Catholic interpretation, because such is impossible in an exegesis that is closely bound up with tradition. The "new" exegesis is opposed rather to the directives of the magisterium and constitutes a danger for the faith that has been handed down to us, not to mention the pernicious effect on young clerics who have come to Rome for their education and formation. I do not intend to give a detailed synopsis of the seventy pages of Romeo's criticism, but a few citations will suffice to reveal its general lines and its polemical tone.

According to Romeo, the very title of Alonso Schökel's article attracted much attention:

> Several bishops, who represent the authentic magisterium of Catholic exegesis, have been perplexed by the question [in the title], because they know better than anyone else where Catholic exegesis should be headed; they would not wish that it be impelled by some group in a direction inconsistent with the traditional doctrine and rich interpretation of the sacred books bequeathed to us by the Fathers and Doctors of the Church and by the "illustrious interpreters of past ages," who "penetrate to the intimate depths of the divine word," nor that it sail too near the subversive or at least adventuresome winds of the "criticism" unleashed by rationalism, which is always of its very nature "intransigent and arrogant." (p. 387)

Introductory pages are devoted to a denunciation of "il progressismo cattolico moderno," a pernicious spirit that must be understood to comprehend the tendency of Alonso Schökel's article, touching, as it does, "the essence of our religion, the legitimacy of the faith that we owe to the Word of God as supreme and immutable apostolic magisterium of the Church" (p. 391).

Romeo insists that he does not "doubt the good faith and the good intentions of Fr. Alonso and of those who are engaged with him in the reform campaign in the area of Catholic exegesis. We are confrères in religion and in the priesthood. If we were to meet and speak together, we would certainly embrace each other" (p. 393). Despite such a manifestation of good will, however, Romeo found it necessary to admit that his own attitude was "even annoying" *(fastidioso)*, for the "matter treated, which is of extreme importance and delicacy, demands it" (p. 396).

Alonso Schökel's viewpoint in the article is said to be explained by his background and his other writings; these are found to be "in agreement with the position that is hostile to tradition and the 'conservatives'" (p. 394). There follows a detailed criticism of many points made by Alonso Schökel in his article. This critique is so extensive that it is impossible to detail it here. The burden of it is summed thus: "No change of direction was perceived in 1943" (p. 409), a flat denial of the *Civiltà Cattolica* article of 1960.

An article of Cardinal A. Bea, S.J., which had been written at the time of the appearance of *Divino afflante Spiritu*, is quoted by Romeo as an "official" interpretation of the encyclical; long excerpts from it are given with footnotes to indicate to what extent Alonso Schökel has disagreed with the mentality of Pius XII and of those responsible for the encyclical (pp. 412–20).

The last part of Alonso Schökel's article is subjected to similar criticism (pp. 420–42): Apropos of it, Romeo writes:

> Either he [Alonso Schökel] does not know the facts, and therefore is an incompetent who should not dare to write for the public on questions treated by a lofty pontifical document, passing judgment on and contradicting affirmations of the Pope, of the great Pius XII, who lavishly endorses, at least as it is attributed to him, the...liberation of Catholic exegesis. Or else he knows the facts, and then we must necessarily be concerned to hinder the systematic defamation or sleight-of-hand treatment *(escamotage)* of the two great encyclicals of the great Pius XII. (p. 425)

The next-to-last part of Romeo's article (pp. 443–50) is devoted to a digression, a complaint attributed to various cardinals, apostolic nuncios, archbishops, bishops, and prelates of the Roman curia, that at present "in various Catholic exegetical circles throughout the whole world the edge of heresy is being grazed and sometimes there is thoroughgoing disbelief." Footnotes 129 and 130 give references to articles in American and French biblical and theological magazines (among them *Theological Studies* and the *Catholic Biblical Quarterly*) that are, in Romeo's opinion, evidence of this tendency. This is supposed to reveal the "undeniable fact of pressure exerted on all the clergy by a group that is working indefatigably *to open* even wider breaches in the superhuman edifice of Catholic faith" (p. 444 [his emphasis]). The entire situation has its roots in the double myth of human liberty and human progress, characteristic of the "new age" *(tempi nuovi)* of the second half of the twentieth century.

The article ends with two observations: Today there does not exist in the bosom of the Catholic Church any danger of obscurantism, fear, or timidity vis-à-vis science or scientific learning. Today's grave and frightening danger is rather that there are manifest within the Church theories and tendencies that threaten to subvert the foundations of Catholic doctrine, over which Pius XII expressed such anxiety, even in the very title of his encyclical *Humani generis:*

> A whole swarm of termites working away incessantly in the shadows, at Rome and in all parts of the world, forces one to take note of the execution of a massive plan of buzzing about and gnawing away at the doctrines that form and nourish our Catholic faith. Ever more numerous signs from various quarters give evidence of the gradual unfolding of a widespread and progressive maneuver, directed by very clever minds, apparently quite pious, which aims at doing away with the Christianity taught up to now and lived for nineteen centuries, in order to substitute for it the Christianity of "the new times." (p. 454)

Enough of an indication of this long article has been given to reveal its tone. Alonso Schökel's discussion of the question "Where is Catholic exegesis headed?" was clearly only an occasion for Romeo. What had disturbed him was not simply that article in *Civiltà Cattolica* but the existence of *a group of exegetes* who seemed to be pushing Catholic interpretation of the Bible in a direction with which he did not agree. In addition to Alonso Schökel's article, he introduced frequent quotations from the writings and lectures of other Catholic exegetes to substantiate his contentions. M. Zerwick, a German

Jesuit and likewise professor at the Biblical Institute in Rome, had addressed a group of some fifty Italian Scripture professors at a meeting in Padua (15–17 September 1959); about a hundred mimeographed copies of his talk were distributed, entitled "Literary Criticism of the NT in the Catholic Exegesis of the Gospels" ("Critica letteraria del N.T. nell'esegesi cattolica dei Vangeli"). In it, Zerwick summarized the conclusions of three other exegetes, A. Vögtle, P. Benoit, O.P., and A. Descamps.[15] From Zerwick's address to the Italian professors, Romeo concluded, "The denial of the historicity of this passage of the first Gospel [Matt 16:16–18] is clear" (p. 436 n. 116). This is but one example of a number of accusations directed against Zerwick throughout the article. The other Catholic exegete frequently referred to in the footnotes in Jean Levie, a Belgian Jesuit, professor of NT studies at Collège Philosophique et Théologique S.J. de Louvain (Eegenhoven) and for many years the editor of *La Nouvelle Revue Théologique*. Romeo found Levie's book, *La Bible: Parole humaine et message de Dieu*,[16] to be "tremendamente eversivo" (tremendously upsetting [p. 444 n. 130]). As he understands Levie, "All of Christianity is to be made over" (p. 455 n. 150). "P. Levie exerted notable influence on P. Alonso, whose professor he seems to have been" (p. 395). Alonso Schökel, Zerwick, and Levie are not the only "religious" who make up the group, for in the course of the footnotes such names occur as C. Spicq, P. Teilhard de Chardin, D. Stanley, and "a close collaborator of P. Alonso," who has been identified as S. Lyonnet.[17]

The follow-up of Romeo's article was also noteworthy. Immediately after his lengthy critique, the same issue of *Divinitas* carried an Italian translation of two chapters that W. F. Albright had contributed to a volume edited by H. H. Rowley, *The Old Testament and Modern Study: A Generation of Discovery and Research*.[18] The translation was preceded, however, by a preface of six pages in italics, which was written to introduce the American Albright to Italian readers, but which ended with a series of references to ecclesiastical documents and was signed by Romeo. The last footnote of that preface quoted the *finis* (purpose) of the Biblical Institute, as set forth by Pius X.[19] The burden of the italicized preface thus became apparent: it was an indirect comparison of what a non-Catholic biblical scholar and archaeologist had to say about the Bible with what the Biblical Institute was supposed to be teaching about it. Such a use of the Italian translation of those chapters was completely unauthorized. The separate printing of the offprints of Romeo's article, which were circulated widely, even went so far as to put the names of Romeo and Albright together on the cover with the title only of Romeo's article.

III

Naturally enough, there ensued a lively reaction to Romeo on the part of the Biblical Institute. Its rector, E. Vogt, a Swiss Jesuit who had worked in southern Brazil, wrote to the editor of *Divinitas*, A. Piolanti, asking for a retractation and for equal space to answer the critique in that magazine. That was refused, and there appeared subsequently in *Verbum Domini* a fifteen-page reply, signed merely as P. I. B. It was entitled, "The Pontifical Biblical Institute and a Recent Booklet of Msgr. A. Romeo."[20] In this article, the Institute complained of the violations of charity involved in the damage done to its reputation through the "very serious...accusations leveled against two professors of this Institute, and this not in private (as has occurred for years now against the Institute), but publicly, and indeed not in an obscure place, but in a magazine that glories in the name *Divinitas*."[21] The article indicated the occasion and source of the accusations, Romeo's methods of "interpreting" his sources, and the most serious accusations (that the professors were opponents of tradition and the magisterium, corruptors of young clerics, teachers of a "double biblical truth," and hypocrites). Each accusation was taken up and refuted.

This controversy took place in Rome — fortunately, for the rest of the Catholic biblical world — and the subsequent developments in such a place were always important to watch. Although the article of Romeo was written by one associated with some of the Vatican congregations, the prefect of the Sacred Congregation of Studies and Universities let it be known at the beginning of February that that article had been published without the knowledge of himself or of the Congregation's secretary and that it represented no more than the ideas of the writer. Moreover, since its tone was so personal, it could in no way be regarded as an official view. On 2 March 1961, the *Osservatore Romano* carried the news that the rector of the Biblical Institute, E. Vogt, S.J., had been named a consultor to the Pontifical Theological

Commission of the coming Vatican Council II. Finally, a letter was sent by A. Miller, O.S.B., the secretary of the Pontifical Biblical Commission, in the name of all the consultors of the Commission who had assembled in the Vatican, to the rector of the Biblical Institute, deprecating the attacks of Msgr. Romeo (mentioned by name) and reaffirming publicly their unshakable solidarity with the Biblical Institute.[22]

IV

Reactions to the controversy appeared in various journals throughout the world. *Herder Korrespondenz* (16/6 [March 1961] 287) was dismayed at the insulting tone of the polemics directed against a biblical confrère, whose orthodoxy was questioned; at the appeal for a censure (as if Rome and the episcopacy were asleep); and at the casting of suspicion on other scholars such as J. Levie, P. Teilhard de Chardin, as well as on American, French, and German journals: "It can scarcely fail to be noted that this article [of Romeo], which is by now certainly known to theologians within and without the Church, is arousing the worst fears of *rabies theologica* [theological witch-hunt]; one would have thought that such a thing did not exist any more. At the present moment this is most regrettable, especially since it originates in Rome itself."

Études ("Rome: ombres et lumières," 308/3 [March 1961] 401) contrasted an optimistic article of C. Boyer ("Il Concilio e l'unità cristiana," *Osservatore Romano*, 21 January 1961, 3), in which the author stressed that, thanks to the Council, "Protestants who are nourished on the Bible will see better how the Roman Church is bound to Sacred Scripture and how it is assured of the assistance of the Holy Spirit to interpret it correctly," with the attack conducted at Rome at present by "tout un clan" against the biblical movement and its scientifically assured results. "If this attack were to succeed and if Catholic exegetes were to lose a sane liberty of research, all hope of useful dialogue with Protestantism would be ruined, perhaps for several decades" (p. 401). J. M. Le Blond in the following issue of *Études* took up an issue for which Romeo had criticized J. Levie.[23] Le Blond regretted the concern for "security" that has been substituted openly for that of truth:

This is the normal mark of integralism; an unquestionably sincere attachment to the Church is compromised by fear, as if the Church had to be afraid of scientific research and the impartial quest for truth. Such "pragmatism" can become very serious and in addition can scarcely offer any confidence to those of our separated brothers whom the proclamation of a council has been leading to look in our direction with greater attention. (p. 85)

Le Blond was much more concerned about the position that the Church was expected to adopt vis-à-vis the "new times" according to Romeo. He takes some of Romeo's statements (such as "The Church has never accommodated herself to what Levie calls history" [456 n. 152]) and contrasts them with statements of Pius XII (Christmas Message, 23 December 1956; *AAS* 49 [1957] 12) and of John XXIII (Allocution to the Students of the Greek College at Rome, 14 June 1959). The latter said:

The Church must adapt herself, since there has been so much evolution in the modern world among the faithful and in the manner of life that they must lead. When she realizes that, she will then turn to her separated brothers and say to them: "See what the Church is, what she has done, how she presents herself." And when the Church appears thus modernized, rejuvenated, she will be able to say to our separated brothers, "Come to us."

Msgr. E. Galbiati, of the Theological Faculty of Milan, found Romeo's article to be a "polemical reply," and since some readers of *Scuola Cattolica* were disturbed by the controversy, he showed how both sides had been trying to remain faithful to the demands of Christian faith.

If at times his [Romeo's] adversaries have given the impression of an excessive security, devoid of any concern about clarifying how their unusual exegesis is nevertheless in accord with or not only in discord with revealed principles, then let it be shown how their security is without foundation and how it cannot be reconciled with the principles admitted by all. The scholarly world expects nothing more than this. But such a hope has been disappointed, for as a result of the violent polemical tone the heart of the matter was never touched, nor was any new light shed on the point at issue.[24]

V

The reaction of the Pontifical Biblical Commission, which has always been looked upon as a guardian of the faith in matters biblical, to the Romeo–Biblical Institute affair was, to say the least, significant. The fact that it sided with the Biblical Institute against the accusations of a Roman monsignor with important connections in various Vatican circles is of much more importance in indicating an official view than any critique of seventy pages.

The Biblical Commission came out in favor of the Biblical Institute in this controversy *in globo*; it reaffirmed its confidence in the professorial staff of that Institute. That does not mean, however, that it agreed with every detail of what was written by the professors in the articles criticized. I note this, not to imply that something amiss was found in such writings, but to present the reaction of the Commission for what it was.

Romeo's article was not just an attack on Alonso Schökel, Zerwick, or the Biblical Institute, but on the whole movement spread widely throughout the Catholic Church of that time. Dedicated Scripture scholars were working seriously in many quarters to further that movement, but their aim was not the destruction of the foundations of Christian faith or the traditions of the Church. Exegetes throughout the world sighed with relief at the news of the reaction of the Biblical Commission to the controversy, for it indicated that official Roman views had not changed since the issuance of the quasi-official explanations of the Secretary of the Biblical Commission and its Under-Secretary in 1955 apropos of its *responsa*.[25]

In this whole controversy, there is a legitimate cause for concern. Though it ensued between two groups of professional exegetes, it was but another manifestation of the regrettable chasm that existed between popular piety and scholarly theology. Some years earlier, J. Lebreton had devoted a lengthy article to a third-century manifestation of such a chasm and its effect on the Church of that time.[26] It would be well to reread that article, even though it is devoted to an entirely different problem, as a background for the understanding of the biblical controversy in Rome in the 1960s.

This account began with an incident in the lives of Jerome and Augustine in order to illustrate how the study of Scripture has ever been fraught with misunderstanding. I would not want to imply that the reactions of the Doctor of Hippo and those of the Roman monsignor were in all respects comparable, but the fear that the Scripture scholars of the world are undermining the faith has appeared before in the history of the Church. The fears of the period of Modernism (the late-nineteenth- and early-twentieth-century phenomenon), however legitimate they might have been, are still known to an older generation of living Scripture scholars today, fears that actually cast a dark cloud over much of Catholic biblical scholarship of the first part of the twentieth century. That cloud was lifted in the appearance of the encyclical of Pius XII in 1943, *Divino afflante Spiritu,* and that day has passed. It is important to recall a celebrated paragraph of that encyclical, of which Alonso Schökel made much in his original article:

> Let all the other sons of the Church bear in mind that the efforts of these resolute laborers in the vineyard of the Lord should be judged not only with equity and justice but also with the greatest charity. All, moreover, should abhor that intemperate zeal that imagines that whatever is new should for that very reason be opposed or suspected. Let them bear in mind above all that in the rules and laws promulgated by the Church there is question of doctrine regarding faith and morals, and that in the immense matter contained in the sacred Books—legislative, historical, sapiential, and prophetical—there are but few texts whose sense has been defined by the authority of the Church; nor are those more numerous about which the teaching of the holy Fathers is unanimous. There are still many points, and some very important, in the discussion and explanation of which the skill and talent of Catholic exegetes can and should be freely exercised

so that each may contribute his part to the advantage of all, to the continued progress of the sacred doctrine, and to the defense and honor of the Church. (§27)[27]

VI

As an aftermath of the Romeo affair, rumors circulated about the preparation by the Holy Office (more recently called the Congregation for the Doctrine of the Faith) of a *monitum* on biblical matters. It was published on 20 June 1961 and appeared in *Osservatore Romano* on 22 June.

Sacred Congregation of the Holy Office

Despite the commendable progress that has been made in the study of the Bible, there are now circulating in various places opinions and affirmations that call into question the genuine historical and objective truth of Sacred Scripture — not only of the Old Testament (as the Sovereign Pontiff Pius XII already deplored in his encyclical *Humani generis*) but also of the New Testament, and even with regard to the words and actions of Jesus Christ.

Such opinions and affirmations create anxieties in the minds of pastors and the faithful. For this reason, the eminent Fathers charged with protecting the doctrine on faith and morals issue a warning to all those who work with the sacred books either orally or in writing. They are to handle such an important issue with the proper degree of prudence and reverence, always keeping in view the teaching of the holy Fathers and the mind and Magisterium of the Church. Otherwise, the consciences of the faithful will be disturbed, and the truths of the faith will suffer harm.

This warning is given with the consent of the eminent Fathers of the Pontifical Biblical Commission.

Sebastianus Masala, *Secretary*[28]

The historical antecedents of this *monitum* have been recounted in the foregoing sections of this essay. It is important not to isolate it from its context. Its first paragraph soberly describes the situation: views and opinions circulating in various regions that call into question the historical truth of Scripture and of the words and deeds of Jesus of Nazareth. As a "warning," it is not an instruction or a decree advocating or condemning any specific view. The first and last clauses of its second paragraph express its predominantly pastoral concern. So important a subject is to be treated with due prudence and reverence.

As a *monitum*, it cannot be regarded as a condemnation of the so-called new direction in biblical studies, of which Alonso Schökel wrote. It would be an error to equate modern biblical studies, which are praised in the first clause, with the circulating "views and opinions"; the caricatures and popularizations of the serious study of Scripture are far more responsible for the problem than solid exegetical work itself. Nor is the *monitum* an accusation leveled specifically against *exegetes*, much less against a "group of *exegetes*" (Romeo's phrase), not to mention the professors of the Biblical Institute, with whom the Biblical Commission earlier expressed its solidarity. It is a warning addressed to "all those who deal with the sacred books either orally or in writing."

It likewise would be an error to isolate the expression *germana veritas historica et obiectiva Scripturae Sacrae* (the genuine historical and objective truth of Sacred Scripture) and argue that the Holy Office was advocating a fundamentalistic approach to the Bible. In using that expression, the Holy Office has not said that *germana veritas* is to be identified with fundamentalistic literalness. The word *germana* (genuine, proper) has been chosen to express the recognition of the kind of truth that is found in Scripture and to allow for its formulation according to various literary genres employed by the sacred writers. It is but another way of saying what Cardinal A. Bea once wrote, "Sua cuique generi literario est veritas" (Each individual genre has its own truth).[29] It is but a brief formulation of what Pius XII wrote about the genres in his encyclical of 1943. The excesses that call such a truth into question were the object of the Holy Office's warning.

The *monitum* also inculcates respect for the interpretation of the Fathers, the *sensus ecclesiae* and its magisterium, for the intention of the warning is clear. It does not, however, negate or qualify what Pius XII stated in his encyclical about the fewness of "texts whose sense has been

35

defined by the authority of the Church" or of those "about which the teaching of the Holy Fathers is unanimous" (see p. 6 above).

Finally, it is apparent that the *monitum* is not to be regarded as a confirmation of Romeo's position. At the end of the text, it is made clear that the warning has been issued with the agreement of the cardinals of the Biblical Commission. That same Commission sided earlier with the Biblical Institute against Romeo. Consequently, there is no reason to look upon the *monitum* as an attempt to change the "new direction" in biblical studies. It is a warning to *all* to treat the Bible with the prudence and reverence required and to respect the usual sources of the Church's teaching authority.

3

THE BIBLICAL COMMISSION'S INSTRUCTION ON THE HISTORICAL TRUTH OF THE GOSPELS

Ever since the publication of the Apostolic Letter of Pope Leo XIII, *Vigilantiae*, which established the Pontifical Biblical Commission in the Catholic Church, it has been regarded as a sort of watchdog or vigilance committee of Catholic biblical studies.[1] To anyone who has followed the activity of that Commission in recent years, it is apparent that it has taken on a much more positive role. Its *responsa* (the so-called decrees) have given way to *instructiones*, which, though they are sometimes occasioned by errors or excessive tendencies in certain biblical matters and contain cautions or warnings, have normally been much more positive and informative in character. Its image, in the Catholic world at least, is no longer that of a vigilance committee, which it once projected. Among many outsiders, however, that image unfortunately is still rather prevalent. In any case, the publication of an Instruction by the Commission in 1964 offered an occasion to see how it was handling a problem that was vexing modern students of the Bible both inside and outside of the Catholic community.

The document of the Commission was entitled *Instructio de historica Evangeliorum veritate*, "Instruction on the Historical Truth of the Gospels."[2] It dealt with a subject that had been the concern of not a few Catholic scholars in recent years. That an age-old problem had been posed in a new form was evident from a *monitum* (Admonition) issued by the Holy Office in June 1961 on the same subject.[3] That document, however, was quite negative in character and tone and shed no light on the problem. The Instruction of the Commission was rather a positive document of no little importance and merited much laudable comment.[4]

That it was a well-nuanced document became evident from newspaper reports announcing its publication. Some of them interpreted it in almost diametrically opposed senses.[5] When it was examined closely, however, it was seen to be a document that did not commit the Catholic student of the Gospels to any fundamentalistic literalness in the matter of their historicity. Nor did it contain a condemnation of any specific modern opinion about the historical value of the Gospels. Although it catalogued in some detail questionable presuppositions of some form critics, this was done to clear the way to a recognition of the value of the method of form criticism itself. The document will be known in history as the first official statement of the Catholic Church that openly countenanced the method and frankly admitted the distinction of three stages of tradition in gospel material, which had emerged from the form-critical study of the Gospels.

Although the document is entitled "An Instruction on the Historical Truth of the Gospels," a close analysis of its text revealed that the most important word in the title was not the adjective "historical," which might have been one's initial impression, but rather the preposition "on" (de). Significantly, par. III,[6] which formulates the problem, omits the word "historical": "...quod multa scripta vulgantur, quibus veritas factorum et dictorum quae in Evangeliis continentur, in discrimen vocatur" (many writings are being spread abroad in which the truth of the deeds and words which are contained in the Gospels is questioned).[7] In light of the rest of the document, the omission of the adjective "historical" seems intentional and therefore noteworthy. In fact, though "historical truth" appears in the title of the Instruction, it is used only once in its text, and that in a sentence in which is decried a certain philosophical or theological presupposition of the form-critical method, to which no Catholic interpreter would subscribe anyway.[8] In none of the positive directives does the term "historical truth" reappear. It is evident, therefore, that the Commission was far more interested in sketching with broad lines the character of gospel truth than in just reasserting that the Gospels were historical.

After three introductory paragraphs, the Commission addressed directives to (a) exegetes, (b) professors of Scripture in seminaries and similar institutions, (c) preachers, (d) those who publish for the faithful, and (e) directors of biblical associations. Under (d) "Ordinaries" (local bishops) were reminded to be vigilant of publications on Scripture. Except for the first case — and this omission may have been a typographical error — the groups addressed were clearly indicated in italics. In the directives addressed to exegetes, italics were used again to indicate the three stages of tradition discussed there. In this way the Instruction has been structured.[9]

Introduction

The Church's concern for Sacred Scripture is recalled as a background for the task of the exegete. He is urged to rely not only on his own resources, but also on God's help and the light of the Church. In par. II, joy is expressed at the growing number of expert interpreters of the Bible in the Church, and an explicit recognition is made of the fact that they have been following papal encouragements. This clause was incorporated undoubtedly to offset the criticism heard at times in some Catholic circles that "exegetes" have been undermining the faith with their "so-called" new interpretations. There follows a counsel to charity, which was needed in this area so peculiarly prone to emotional discussions. It repeats the counsels of the encyclical *Divino afflante Spiritu* and of the Apostolic Letter *Vigilantiae*. Tucked away between the quotations is the remark that not even Jerome was always successful in handling scriptural difficulties in his day. Paragraph III sets forth the problem and states the Commission's purpose in issuing the Instruction.

To the Exegetes

Eight of the remaining fifteen paragraphs of the Instruction have been addressed to exegetes (par. IV–XI), and when they are compared with the rest, it is evident that the essential directives of the Instruction are found here; for the directives to seminary professors, preachers, popular writers, and directors of biblical associations are hortatory and prudential. There are, of course, exhortations and cautions addressed to exegetes, but it is only in these eight paragraphs of the Instruction that one finds directives of a positive doctrinal nature.[10]

Paragraph IV contains an exhortation addressed to the *Catholic exegete,* who is counseled to derive profit from all the contributions of former interpreters, especially from the Fathers and Doctors of the Church — in this, following the example of the Church itself. He is, however, to utilize also norms of "rational and Catholic hermeneutics." What is meant here, apparently, by "rational" hermeneutics is the generally admitted norms of criticism, which prevail in all branches of literature. Such would be the norms of literary and historical criticism that guide any philologian or interpreter of ancient documents or literature. The addition of "Catholic" defines further norms that must guide the Catholic interpreter (e.g., that the Bible is a collection of inspired writings, that revelation is contained in them, that a certain number of texts have a traditional meaning resolving the "open," indecisive sense that at times is all that can be arrived at by philological analysis, etc.). What is specifically meant by the norms of rational and Catholic hermeneutics is indicated further by the recommendation of the aids offered by the historical method. Next, the Commission urges the exegete once again to study the literary form used by the sacred writer and recalls the words of Pope Pius XII that this is the exegete's duty and that it may not be neglected.[11] The last sentence of par. IV, urging the study of the nature of the gospel testimony, outlines in brief the bulk of the directives addressed to the exegetes (in par. VII–X).

Paragraph V is a statement about the use of the form-critical method in the study of the Gospels. It clearly distinguishes what the Commission called the "reasonable elements" *(sana elementa)* in the method itself from its questionable "philosophical and theological principles." Such presuppositions often had come to be mixed with the method and tended to vitiate the conclusions drawn by it. This is not the place to explain in detail the method or its defective presuppositions.[12] One need only note the six specific "principles" listed in the Instruction that are rejected by Catholic exegetes. The six presuppositions listed are: (a) denial of a supernatural order; (b) denial of God's intervention in the world in strict revelation; (c) denial of the possibility and existence of miracles (the first three are inheritances from rationalism); (d) incompatibility of faith with historical truth; (e) an almost a priori denial of the historical value and nature of the documents of revelation; and (f) a disdain for apostolic testimony and undue emphasis on the creative community in the early Church.[13]

Having made this distinction between the "reasonable elements" and the "philosophical and theological principles" of the form-critical method, the Commission proceeds in par. VI to make use of another distinction, which is really the fruit of a sane use of the method applied to the Gospels. In fact, it merely applies a distinction that had been in use for some time among exegetes, both Catholic and non-Catholic, which enables one to evaluate "the nature of gospel testimony, the religious life of the early Churches, and the sense and value of apostolic tradition" (par. IV).

The "three stages of tradition" *(tria tempora traditionis)* have been called by other names, and this may be a bit confusing at first. However, the different terminology brings out other aspects of the problem, and in some cases it is due to the historical development of the form-critical debate itself. Some writers speak of the three levels of comprehension according to which the gospel text is to be understood. Others speak of the three contexts of gospel material. In the latter case, the expression is a development of the original idea of the *Sitz im Leben* (life setting) of the German form critics. The pioneers who made use of this method after the First World War sought to assign to the various stories in the Gospels a *Sitz im Leben*, i.e., a vital context that would explain the formation of the story. For these pioneers, *Sitz im Leben* meant *Sitz im Leben der Kirche*, "a setting in the life of the Church." In time, as the debate developed, the question arose about the *Sitz im Leben Jesu*, the vital context in the ministry of Jesus, in which the saying or episode might have had its origin in some form or other. To capture this setting with any certainty, however, is a very delicate and difficult activity. Finally, there was modeled on these two *Sitze im Leben* a third, which is only analogous. Granted that questions about the vital context in the early Church or in Jesus' ministry might be legitimate and instructive; nevertheless, in the long run the important thing is the *Sitz im Evangelium*, the gospel context of the saying or narrated event. How did the evangelist make use of traditional material that he had inherited? Despite the names that one might prefer for these three stages and the nuances that such differences in terminology might suggest, they are all in the long run saying the same thing: to understand what the inspired, canonical Gospels tell us about the life, ministry, and teaching of Jesus of Nazareth, one

41

has to make an important threefold distinction. Paragraph VI states this in a topic sentence.

Paragraph VII begins with the italicized words *Christus Dominus…*, using of him titles that are more properly characteristic of the second stage. It would have been better to speak here of *Jesus Nazarenus*. At any rate, it deals with the *Sitz im Leben Jesu*, with the things that Jesus actually did and said, with the things that the chosen disciples saw and heard. Two things are emphasized: what the disciples saw and heard fitted them to give testimony about Jesus' life and teaching; and the accommodations that Jesus made in his teaching were intended so that it would be understood and retained. The first few statements in the paragraph are documented with references to the NT. The rest of it is a speculative reconstruction, slightly idyllic, but undoubtedly expressing what is essentially to be recalled about this first stage of the tradition.

It is the stage of the *ipsissima verba Jesu*, and for Christians it has always seemed to be the stage of greatest importance. What Jesus himself really said would be more important than what the early Church passed on as his teaching or what the evangelists recorded as his sayings. And yet, it is noteworthy that the Commission did not insist in any way that what we have in the Gospels is a record of this first stage of the tradition.

The second stage of the tradition is dealt with in par. VIII. Once again, the emphasis is on the testimony of the apostles and the accommodations that they made in their message to the needs of those to whom they preached. Even when the Commission says that the apostles after the resurrection "faithfully explained his life and words," it significantly appeals to none of the Gospels, but to one of the speeches of Peter in Acts 10:36–41. This speech gives a summary of the life and ministry of Christ, and it has been regarded by C. H. Dodd and others as an example of the early Church's kerygmatic preaching.[14] It has often been thought that Mark, the earliest of the canonical Gospels, is an expansion of such a summary. Yet it is noteworthy that there are no "words" of Jesus quoted in Peter's speech; and yet such a speech is regarded as a faithful explanation of Jesus' "life and words." This important nuance should not be missed.

The Commission is rightly at pains in this section to counteract the idea that the new faith of the apostles after the resurrection and the pentecostal experience should be thought of as having destroyed any recollections of Jesus' ministry that the apostles had or as having deformed their impression of him, volatilizing him into some sort of "mythical" person.

Even though such an idea is rejected, the Commission insists that the apostles passed on what Jesus had said and done "with that fuller understanding which they enjoyed" as a result of the experiences they went through at the first Easter and the illumination of the Spirit of Truth at the first Christian Pentecost. Obvious examples of this fuller understanding are cited from the Johannine Gospel (2:22; 12:16; 11:51–52). These instances in the sacred text are identified explicitly, but the Commission gives no indication that this fuller understanding is limited to the three passages only. For the accommodation to the needs of the audiences, on which stress is put, must have often made the apostles rephrase sayings and recast their stories. Certainly, some of the differences in the Synoptic tradition are owing to this sort of accommodation, which affected the oral tradition in the preliterary stage — no matter how much leeway one may want to allow the evangelists themselves in the third stage of the tradition.

Paragraph VIII ends with the mention of the "various modes of speaking" that the apostles used in their ministry and preaching. Because they had to speak to "Greeks and barbarians, the wise and the foolish," such contact and influence naturally caused an adaptation of the message they were proclaiming. It is made clear that the "literary forms" employed in such adaptation had to be distinguished and properly assessed *(distinguendi et perpendendi)*. This formulation leaves no doubt that the Commission had in mind the use of the form-critical method. However, the forms that are mentioned specifically ("catecheses, stories,[15] testimonia, hymns, doxologies, prayers") are found, indeed, in the NT, but it is another question whether they all are used in the Gospels, at least in any abundance. Nevertheless, the point is made that various literary forms did develop at this stage of the Christian tradition, and that the student of the Gospels must distinguish them and assess them. Still more important is the admission by the Commission that there are other forms not specifically mentioned *(aliaeque id genus formae litterariae)* such as were used by writers of that time. As far as the Gospels are concerned, one thinks readily of genealogies, parables, miracle stories, and midrash.

The longest discussion is devoted to the third stage of the gospel tradition in par. IX. Striking is the emphasis that is laid here on the evangelists' "method suited to the peculiar purpose which each one set for himself." The Commission reckons with a process of selection, synthesis, and explication at this stage of the tradition. Adaptation to the needs of readers also influenced this process. Because the evangelist often transposed episodes from one context to another, the exegete must seek out the meaning intended by the evangelist in narrating a saying or deed in a certain way or putting it in a different context. In saying this, the Commission implicitly countenances a form of *Redaktionsgeschichte*. This is a phase of modern gospel study that superseded form criticism *(Formgeschichte)*. Whereas the latter is interested in the history of the literary form and its genesis, *Redaktionsgeschichte* studies rather the "redactional history" of an episode: how the evangelist-compiler has edited or made use of the inherited material in his composition.

After such an exhortation to the exegete to seek out *the evangelist's meaning,* the Commission makes a statement about the "truth" involved in such a process of redaction. "For the truth of the story [or narrative, if one insists] is not affected by the fact that the evangelists relate the words and deeds of the Lord in a different order and express his sayings not literally, but differently, while preserving their sense." The Commission speaks of "truth" only and does not specify it as "historical truth." One might wonder what it would mean if the word "historical" were to be understood here, after such an admission of the redactional work of the evangelists. If one were to ask, however, "Well, then, if it is not a question of historical truth, of what kind is it?" the answer would have to be, "of the gospel truth." Paragraph X will, I think, bear this out. The quotation from St. Augustine at the end of the paragraph, even though it comes from a writer who held a less sophisticated view of the Gospels than the Commission's Instruction is advocating, is nevertheless nuanced enough to be pertinent.

At the end of this discussion of the threefold stages of the gospel tradition, the Commission notes that the exegete will not be fulfilling his task unless he pays careful attention to all these facets of the gospel tradition. It implies that this distinction is the result of the "laudable achievements of recent research." Then comes the significant statement:

From the results of the new investigations it is apparent that the doctrine and the life of Jesus were not simply reported for the sole purpose of being remembered, but were "preached" so as to offer the Church a basis of faith and of morals. The interpreter (then), by tirelessly scrutinizing the testimony of the evangelists, will be able to illustrate more profoundly the perennial theological value of the Gospels and bring out clearly how necessary and important the Church's interpretation is.[16]

The Commission implies, then, that the gospel truth is not something that is tied up with any fundamentalistic literalness.

The last paragraph addressed to the exegetes (par. XI) begins with an admission that there are still many serious problems on which the exegete "can and must freely exercise his skill and genius." This admission is a repetition of a statement of Pius XII about the liberty of the Catholic exegete. The statement, however, is paraphrased, and a significant addition to it spells out the relationship of the work of exegetes in the Church to that of the magisterium. I juxtapose the two texts:

Divino afflante Spiritu §25	*Instruction*
There are still many points, and some very important, in the discussion and explanation of which the skill and talent of Catholic exegetes can and should be freely exercised, so that each may contribute his part to the advantage of all, to the continued progress of sacred doctrine,	There are still many things, and of the greatest importance, in the discussion and explanation of which the Catholic exegete can and must freely exercise his skill and genius, so that each may contribute his part to the advantage of all, to the continued progress of sacred doctrine, to the preparation and further support of the judgment to be exercised by the ecclesiastical magisterium, and to the defense
and to the defense and honor of the Church.[17]	and honor of the Church.

The exegete is urged further to be ready to submit to the directives of the magisterium, never to forget that the apostles preached the good news, and the evangelists were inspired and so were preserved "from all error." This is supported by a quotation from St. Irenaeus. So end the directives to exegetes.

To Professors of Scripture in Seminaries and Similar Institutions

The directives addressed to Scripture professors in seminaries and similar institutions (par. XII) consist of an exhortation to teach Scripture in a way that the dignity of the subject and the needs of the times require. Coming immediately after the directives to exegetes, who have once again been enjoined to study the literary forms and encouraged to pursue the form-critical method in the interpretation of the Gospels, this exhortation implies the seminary professor's duty to cope with the same. In this day and age, professors cannot afford to ignore them. The Commission insists, however, that the use of such a method of literary criticism is not an end in itself. It is to be used to bring out the sense of the Gospel passage intended by God through what the human author has written. The professor is above all to emphasize the theological teaching of the Gospels, and the literary criticism serves only to bring out the theology of the evangelists. Those whom the professor is training are future priests, for whose lives and work the Scriptures must be the source of perennial vitality. This exhortation is predominantly positive in tone; the only negative element in it is the warning against the pursuit of literary criticism as if it were an end in itself.

To Preachers

In the case of preachers, the Biblical Commission first insists on their preaching of "doctrine," appealing to 1 Tim 4:16 (par. XIII). The first strong negative directive of the Instruction appears here: "They are to refrain entirely from proposing vain and insufficiently established novelties." This prohibition must be understood properly, however, for immediately afterwards the Commission allows for the cautious explanation of "new opinions already solidly established."

The problem is obvious. There cannot be a double standard of truth, one for exegetes and Scripture professors, and another for the faithful. If I am correct in my estimate of this Instruction, the recognition that the Biblical Commission gives to literary forms, and especially to the form-critical method of Gospel interpretation, would put interpretations based on this method among those solidly established "new opinions," which may be explained to the faithful. The directives for preachers end with another caution: they are not to embellish biblical episodes with imaginative details not consonant with the truth.

To Those Who Publish for the Faithful

The same prudence demanded of preachers is now required of all those who write on biblical subjects at a popular level (par. XIV). They are to concentrate on the riches of God's Word and are to consider it a sacred duty never to depart from the common teaching and tradition of the Church. They may exploit, however, the findings of modern biblical research, but avoid "the rash comments of innovators." A "pernicious itch for newness" is not to lead them to disseminate rashly what are only trial solutions to classic difficulties of the sacred text. The Commission recalls that books and articles on biblical subjects in magazines and newspapers are to be scrutinized carefully by Ordinaries (local bishops) (par. XV).

To Biblical Associations

The directors of biblical associations are to follow the norms for such gatherings already laid down by the Biblical Commission.

Conclusion

The Biblical Commission notes in conclusion that, if all these directives are followed, the study of Sacred Scripture can only contribute to the benefit of the faithful. It ends with a quotation from 2 Tim 3:15–17.

Final Remarks

The significance of this 1964 Instruction of the Biblical Commission is comprehended best when one considers the events that had been taking place within Roman Catholic circles. I am not referring directly to the strife between the Lateran University and the Biblical Institute in Rome, which was unfortunate because it obscured the issue of the Church's attitude toward an important biblical problem.[18] Rather, I have in mind the mixed reactions that had been reported all over the world to the new trends in modem Catholic biblical studies ever since the 1943 encyclical of Pius XII, *Divino afflante Spiritu*, and how attempts were made in conservative ecclesiastical circles (in Rome and elsewhere) to commit the Catholic interpretation of the Gospel narratives to a fundamentalistic reading of them.[19] In this context, the well-nuanced position that the Commission has taken in this Instruction has been and is of great importance. In effect, it has given official sanction to many of the new trends in biblical studies.[20]

The silence of the Commission about certain matters, however, raised several questions. First of all, practically nothing has been said in the Instruction about the so-called Synoptic Problem. In dealing with the redactional work of the evangelists, the Instruction admits that they used a "method suited to the peculiar purpose which each set for himself," and selected, synthesized, transposed, etc. It seems rather obvious that the Commission did not want to take sides in the debate about the solution of this problem (whether one follows the classic Two-Source theory, or a modified form of it, or even the less likely Griesbach hypothesis or theories of oral tradition). This has been a knotty question, and one that probably will never be solved to the satisfaction of everybody. The Instruction has left the debate on this issue open, but its silence makes some of its statements sound like an oversimplification of the situation. To non-Catholic students of the Gospels, this reaction will be the first to come to mind. How can one discuss the problem of the historical value of the gospel tradition without assuming some position on the Synoptic Problem? One can only speculate about the reason for the silence of the Commission: it apparently thought it could give directives in a generic enough fashion that would not tend to close the debate about the solution to the Problem.

Second, there is the question of the reinterpretation of the words of Jesus by the evangelists in their redactional work. In recent times, it has been suggested often that the evangelists put on the lips of Jesus a fuller form of his sayings than the *ipsissima verba* or that certain verses are to be regarded even as the redactional additions of the evangelists. To cite a few examples, the Matthean additions to the Beatitudes,[21] to the Our Father, the "exceptive" clauses in the divorce texts, and even the very knotty problem of Matthew 16:16b–19.[22] Significantly, the Commission has not come out against such views in Catholic biblical studies in an otherwise comprehensive statement on the "historical truth of the Gospels." The Commission has admitted the redactional activity of the evangelists (par. IX), and it may even be hinting at the *kind* of redaction that this question of the reinterpretation of the words of Jesus calls for, when it says, "From the many things handed down, they selected some things, reduced others to a synthesis, *(still) others they explicated as they kept in mind the situation of the Churches*" (par. IX [my emphasis]).[23] Such an unfolding, explanation, or explication of traditional matter for the guidance of local Churches has to be reckoned with. Several writers have appealed to this type of "explanation" for the peculiar addition of the "exceptive" clauses in the divorce texts of Matt 5:32 and 19:9.[24] The evangelist would have added these words because of a problem in the early Jewish-Christian community, echoes of which are found in Acts 15:20, 29 and 21:25. The Commission's statements, however, are not explicit enough to say that it expressly countenanced the assertion of such redactional activity on the part of evangelists; but it is not excluded either. Its silence, therefore, on this issue — which is really crucial today — is eloquent.

When all is said and done, the most significant thing in the whole Instruction is that the Biblical Commission calmly and frankly admitted that what is contained in the Gospels as we have them today is not the words and deeds of Jesus in the first stage of the gospel tradition (roughly corresponding to A.D. 1–33), and not even the form in which they were preached in the second stage (= A.D. 33–65), but only in the form compiled and edited by the evangelists in stage three (= A.D. 65–95). This form, of course, reflects the two previous stages, and the second more than the first. So it is good to recall that the redacted form of the sayings and deeds of Jesus that the evangelists give us is the inspired form, but it is not a stenographic report of an

49

eyewitness. The evangelists were inspired by the Holy Spirit to compile and write down the accounts as they did. This inspiration guarantees their gospel truth, which is free from error. It is also good to recall that neither the Church in her official pronouncements on the nature of inspiration, nor the theologians in their speculative treatments of it, have taught that the necessary formal effect of inspiration is historicity. The consequence of inspiration is inerrancy, i.e., immunity from formal error in what is affirmed or asserted. The opposite of error is not simply historicity but truth. There is, however, poetical truth as well as historical truth, rhetorical truth as well as legal truth, mythical truth as well as gospel truth. If a passage in the Gospels contains historical truth, it does not contain it simply because it is inspired. The reasons for its historicity will be quite other than the inspired character of the text. The inspiration may guarantee such historical truth as is there, but it will not guarantee it any more than it would guarantee the poetic truth of the hymn to Christ in Philippians 2. Its guarantee is not quantitative but qualitative and analogous. The inspired truth was intended by God to give human beings not simply a "remembered" account of the doctrine and life of Jesus, but a "preached" form of it, "so as to offer the Church a basis of faith and of morals" (par. X).[25]

The Instruction of the Biblical Commission has not put an end to all the problems regarding the historicity of the Gospels. Discussion of them has continued and will continue, but now with more freedom.

The Text of the Instruction

I. Holy Mother the Church, "the pillar and bulwark of truth"* has always used Sacred Scripture in her task of imparting heavenly salvation to human beings. She has always defended it, too, from every sort of false interpretation. Since there will never be an end to (biblical) problems, the Catholic exegete should never lose heart in explaining the divine word and in solving the difficulties proposed to him. Rather, let him strive earnestly to open up still more the real meaning of the Scriptures. Let him rely firmly not only on his own resources, but above all on the help of God and the light of the Church.

* For the text of the Instruction in this section, note reference numbers are Roman numerals, and the notes appear at the end of this chapter.

II. It is a source of great joy that there are found today, to meet the needs of our times, faithful sons of the Church in great numbers who are experts in biblical matters. They are following the exhortations of the Supreme Pontiffs and are dedicating themselves whole-heartedly and untiringly to this serious and arduous task. "Let all the other sons of the Church bear in mind that the efforts of these resolute laborers in the vineyard of the Lord are to be judged not only with equity and justice, but also with the greatest charity,"[ii] since even illustrious interpreters, such as Jerome himself, tried at times to explain the more difficult questions with no great success.[iii] Care should be had "that the keen strife of debate should never exceed the bounds of mutual charity. Nor should the impression be given in an argument that truths of revelation and divine traditions are being called in question. For unless agreement among minds be safeguarded and principles be carefully respected, great progress in this discipline will never be expected from the diverse pursuits of so many persons."[iv]

III. Today more than ever the work of exegetes is needed, because many writings are being spread abroad in which the truth of the deeds and words that are contained in the Gospels is questioned. For this reason the Pontifical Biblical Commission, in pursuit of the task given to it by the Supreme Pontiffs, has considered it proper to set forth and insist upon the following points.

IV. 1. Let the Catholic exegete, following the guidance of the Church, derive profit from all that earlier interpreters, especially the holy Fathers and Doctors of the Church, have contributed to the understanding of the sacred text. Let him carry on their labors still further. In order to put the abiding truth and authority of the Gospels in their full light, he will accurately adhere to the norms of rational and Catholic hermeneutics. He will diligently employ the new exegetical aids, above all those which the historical method, taken in its widest sense, offers to him — a method which carefully investigates sources and defines their nature and value, and makes use of such helps as textual criticism, literary criticism, and the study of languages. The interpreter will heed the advice of Pius XII of happy memory, who enjoined him "prudently...to examine what contribution the manner of expression or the literary form used by the sacred writer makes to a true and genuine interpretation. And let him be convinced that this part of his task cannot be neglected without serious detriment to

Catholic exegesis."ᵛ By this piece of advice Pius XII enunciated a general rule of hermeneutics by which the books of the Old Testament as well as the New must be explained. For in composing them the sacred writers employed the way of thinking and writing that was in vogue among their contemporaries. Finally, the exegete will use all the means available to probe more deeply into the nature of gospel testimony, the religious life of the early Churches, and the sense and the value of apostolic tradition.

V. As occasion warrants, the interpreter may examine what reasonable elements are contained in the "form-critical method" that can be used for a fuller understanding of the Gospels. But let him be wary, because scarcely admissible philosophical and theological principles have often come to be mixed with this method, which not uncommonly have vitiated the method itself as well as the conclusions in the literary area. For some proponents of this method have been led astray by the prejudiced views of rationalism. They refuse to admit the existence of a supernatural order and the intervention of a personal God in the world through strict revelation, and the possibility and existence of miracles and prophecies. Others begin with a false idea of faith, as if it had nothing to do with historical truth — or rather were incompatible with it. Others deny the historical value and nature of the documents of revelation almost a priori. Finally, others make light of the authority of the apostles as witnesses to Christ, and of their task and influence in the primitive community, extolling rather the creative power of that community. All such views are not only opposed to Catholic doctrine, but are also devoid of scientific basis and alien to the correct principles of historical method.

VI. 2. To judge properly concerning the reliability of what is transmitted in the Gospels, the interpreter should pay diligent attention to the three stages of tradition by which the doctrine and life of Jesus have come down to us.

VII. *Christ our Lord* joined to himself chosen disciples,ᵛⁱ who followed him from the beginning,ᵛⁱⁱ saw his deeds, heard his words, and in this way were equipped to be witnesses of his life and doctrine.ᵛⁱⁱⁱ When the Lord was orally explaining his doctrine, he followed the modes of reasoning and of exposition that were in vogue at the time. He accommodated himself to the mentality of his listeners and saw to it that what he taught was impressed firmly on the mind and easily remembered by the disciples. These men understood the miracles and other events of the life of Jesus correctly, as deeds performed or designed that people might believe in Christ through them and embrace with faith the doctrine of salvation.

VIII. The *apostles* proclaimed above all the death and resurrection of the Lord, as they bore witness to Jesus.[ix] They faithfully explained his life and words,[x] while taking into account in their method of preaching the circumstances in which their listeners found themselves.[xi] After Jesus rose from the dead and his divinity was clearly perceived,[xii] faith, far from destroying the memory of what had transpired, rather confirmed it, because their faith rested on the things that Jesus did and taught.[xiii] Nor was he changed into a "mythical" person and his teaching deformed in consequence of the worship, which the disciples from that time on paid Jesus as the Lord and the Son of God. There is no reason to deny, however, that the apostles passed on to their listeners what was really said and done by the Lord with that fuller understanding that they enjoyed,[xiv] having been instructed by the glorious events of the Christ and taught by the light of the Spirit of Truth.[xv] So, just as Jesus himself after his resurrection "interpreted to them"[xvi] the words of the Old Testament as well as his own,[xvii] they too interpreted his words and deeds according to the needs of their listeners. "Devoting themselves to the ministry of the word,"[xviii] they preached and made use of various modes of speaking that were suited to their own purpose and the mentality of their listeners. For they were debtors[xix] "to Greeks and barbarians, to the wise and the foolish."[xx] But these modes of speaking with which the preachers proclaimed Christ must be distinguished and (properly) assessed: catecheses, stories, testimonia, hymns, doxologies, prayers — and other literary forms of this sort that were in Sacred Scripture and were accustomed to be used by people of that time.

IX. This primitive instruction, which was passed on at first by word of mouth and then in writing — for it soon happened that many tried "to compile a narrative of the things"[xxi] that concerned the Lord Jesus — was committed to writing by the *sacred authors* in four Gospels for the benefit of the Churches, with a method suited to the peculiar purpose that each (author) set for himself. From the many things handed down, they selected some things, reduced others to a synthesis, (still) others they explicated as they kept in mind the situation of the Churches. With every (possible) means they sought that their readers might become aware of the reliability[xxii] of those words, by which they had been instructed. Indeed, from what they had received the sacred writers above all selected the things that were suited to the various situations of the faithful and to the purposes that they had in mind, and adapted their narration of them to the same situations and purpose. Since the meaning of a statement also depends on the sequence, the evangelists, in passing on the word and deeds of our Saviour, explained these now in one context, now in another, depending on (their) usefulness to the readers. Consequently, let the exegete seek out the meaning intended by the evangelist in narrating a saying or a deed in a certain way or in placing it in a certain context. For the truth of the story is not at all affected by the fact that the evangelists related the words and deeds of the Lord in a different order,[xxiii] and expressed his sayings not literally but differently, while preserving (their) sense.[xxiv] For, as St. Augustine says, "It is quite probable that the evangelist believed it to have been his duty to recount what he had to in that order in which it pleased God to suggest it to his memory — in those things at least in which the order, whether it be this or that, detracts in nothing from the truth and authority of the Gospel. But why the Holy Spirit, who apportions individually to each one as he wills,[xxv] and who therefore undoubtedly also governed and ruled the minds of the holy (writers) in recalling what they were to write because of the preeminent authority that the books were to enjoy, permitted one to compile his narrative in this way, and another in that, anyone with pious diligence may seek the reason and with divine aid will be able to find it."[xxvi]

X. Unless the exegete pays attention to all these things that pertain to the origin and composition of the Gospels and makes proper use of all the laudable achievements of recent research, he will not fulfill his task of probing into what the sacred writers intended and what they really said. From the results of the new investigations, it is apparent that the doctrine and life of Jesus were not simply reported for the sole purpose of being remembered, but were "preached" so as to offer the Church a basis of faith and of morals. The interpreter (then), by tirelessly scrutinizing the testimony of the evangelists, will be able to illustrate more profoundly the perennial theological value of the Gospels and bring out clearly how necessary and important the Church's interpretation is.

XI. There are still many things, and of the greatest importance, in the discussion and explanation of which the Catholic exegete can and must freely exercise his skill and genius so that each many contribute his part to the advantage of all, to the continued progress of sacred doctrine, to the preparation and further support of the judgment to be exercised by the ecclesiastical magisterium, and to the defense and honor of the Church.[xxvii] But let him always be disposed to obey the magisterium of the Church, and not forget that the apostles, filled with the Holy Spirit, preached the good news, and that the Gospels were written under the inspiration of the Holy Spirit, who preserved their authors from all error. "Now we have not learned of the plan of our salvation from any others than those through whom the gospel has come to us. Indeed, what they once preached, they later passed to us in the Scriptures by the will of God, as the ground and pillar of our faith. It is not right to say that they preached before they had acquired perfect knowledge, as some would venture to say who boast of being correctors of the apostles. In fact, after our Lord rose from the dead and they were invested with power from on high, as the Holy Spirit came upon them, they were filled with all (his) gifts and had perfect knowledge. They went forth to the ends of the earth, one and all with God's gospel, announcing the news of God's bounty to us and proclaiming heavenly peace to people."[xxviii]

XII. 3. Those whose task it is to *teach in seminaries and similar institutions* should have it as their "prime concern that...Holy Scripture be so taught as both the dignity of the discipline and the needs of the times require."[xxix] Let the teachers above all explain its theological teaching, so that the Sacred Scriptures "may become for the future priests of the Church both a pure and never-failing source for their own spiritual life, as well as food and strength for the sacred task of preaching, which they are about to undertake."[xxx] When they practice the art of criticism, especially so-called literary criticism, let them not pursue it as an end in itself, but that through it they might more plainly perceive the sense intended by God through the sacred writer. Let them not stop, therefore, halfway, content only with their literary discoveries, but show in addition how these things really contribute to a clearer understanding of revealed doctrine, or, if it be the case, to the refutation of errors. Instructors who follow these norms will enable their students to find in Sacred Scripture that which can "raise the mind to God, nourish the soul, and further the interior life."[xxxi]

XIII. 4. Those *who instruct the Christian people in sacred sermons* have need of great prudence. Let them above all pass on doctrine, mindful of St. Paul's warning, "Look to yourself and your teaching; hold on to that. For by so doing, you will save both yourself and those who listen to you."[xxxii] They are to refrain entirely from proposing vain or insufficiently established novelties. As for new opinions already solidly established, they may explain them, if need be, but with caution and due care for their listeners. When they narrate biblical events, let them not add imaginative details that are not consonant with the truth.

XIV. This virtue of prudence should be cherished especially by *those who publish for the faithful.* Let them carefully bring forth the heavenly riches of the divine word "that the faithful may be moved and inflamed rightly to conform their lives (to them)."[xxxiii] They should consider it a sacred duty never to depart in the slightest degree from the common doctrine and tradition of the Church. They should indeed exploit all the real advances of biblical science, which the diligence of recent (scholars) has produced, but they are to avoid entirely the rash remarks of innovators.[xxxiv] They are strictly forbidden to disseminate, led on by some pernicious itch for newness, any trial solutions for difficulties without a prudent selection and serious discrimination, for thus they perturb the faith of many.

XV. This Pontifical Biblical Commission has already considered it proper to recall that books and articles in magazines and newspapers are subject to the authority and jurisdiction of Ordinaries, since they treat of religious matters and pertain to the religious instruction of the faithful.[xxxv] Ordinaries are therefore requested to keep watch with great care over popular writings of this sort.

XVI. 5. Those who are in charge of biblical associations are to comply faithfully with the norms laid down by the Pontifical Biblical Commission.[xxxvi]

XVII. If all these things are observed, the study of Sacred Scripture will contribute to the benefit of the faithful. Even in our time, everyone realizes the wisdom of what St. Paul wrote: The Sacred Writings "can instruct (us) for salvation through faith in Christ Jesus.

All Scripture is divinely inspired and profitable for teaching, for reproof, for correction, and for training in uprightness, so that the man of God may be perfect, equipped for every good work."xxxvii

XVIII. The Holy Father, Pope Paul VI, at the audience graciously granted to the undersigned secretary on 21 April, 1964, approved this Instruction and ordered the publication of it.

> *Rome, 21 April 1964*
> Benjamin N. Wambacq, O.Praem.
> *Secretary of the Commission*

Notes to "The Text of the Instruction"

   i. 1 Tim 3:15. (Notes i–xxxvii correspond to notes 1–37 of the Latin text in general; occasionally it has been necessary to reverse two of them because of the English wording. Words added in parentheses do not appear in the Latin text; they have been supplied for the sake of the English idiom. For some strange reason, references to the encyclical *Divino afflante Spiritu* are given in the Latin text of the Instruction to the Italian translation of the encyclical in *AAS*. I have changed them to the corresponding pages of the official Latin text of the encyclical.)
   ii. *DaS* 47 (*AAS* 35 [1943] 319; *EB* §564; Béchard, SD, 132 [§25]).
   iii. Cf. *Spiritus Paraclitus* 2,3 (*EB* §451; Béchard, SD, 81–111[?]).
   iv. Leo XIII, Apostolic Letter, *Vigilantiae* (*EB* §143; Béchard, SD, 65 [§8]).
   v. *DaS* 38 (*AAS* 35 [1943] 316; *EB* §560; Béchard, SD, 129–30 [§21]).
   vi. Mark 3:14; Luke 6:13.
   vii. Luke 1:2; Acts 1:21–22.
   viii. Luke 24:48; John 15:27; Acts 1:8; 10:39; 13:31.
   ix. Luke 24:44–48; Acts 2:32; 3:15; 5:30–32.
   x. Acts 10:36–41.
   xi. Compare Acts 13:16–41 with Acts 17:22–31.
   xii. Acts 2:36; John 20:28.
   xiii. Acts 2:22; 10:37–39.
   xiv. John 2:22; 12:16; 11:51–52; cf. 14:26; 16:12–13; 7:39.
   xv. John 14:26; 16:13.
   xvi. Luke 24:47.
   xvii. Luke 24:44–45; Acts 1:3.
   xviii. Acts 6:4.

xix. 1 Cor 9:19–23.

xx. Rom 1:14.

xxi. Luke 1:1.

xxii. Luke 1:4.

xxiii. Cf. John Chrysostom, *Hom. in Matth.* 1.3 (PG 57:16–17).

xxiv. Augustine, *De consensu evangelistarum* 2.12.28 (*PL* 34:1090–91; *CSEL* 43:127–29).

xxv. 1 Cor 12:11.

xxvi. Augustine, *De consensu evangelistarum* 2.21.51–52 (*PL* 34:1102; *CSEL* 43:153).

xxvii. *DaS* 47 (*AAS* 35 [1943] 319; *EB* §565; Béchard, *SD*, 132 [§25]).

xxviii. Irenaeus, *Adversus haereses* 3.1.1 (Harvey 2.2; *PG* 7:844).

xxix. Pius X, Apostolic Letter, *Quoniam in re biblica* (*EB* §162; Béchard, *SD*, 67).

xxx. *DaS* 55 (*AAS* 35 [1943] 1322; *EB* §567; Béchard, *SD*, 134 [§27]).

xxxi. *DaS* 25 (*AAS* 35 [1943] 311; *EB* §552; Béchard, *SD*, 125 [§16]).

xxxii. 1 Tim 4:16.

xxxiii. *DaS* 50 (*AAS* 35 [1943] 320; *EB* §566; Béchard, *SD*, 136 [§29]).

xxxiv. Pius X, Apostolic Letter, *Quoniam in re biblica* 13 (*EB* §175; Béchard, *SD*, 69).

xxxv. Instruction *De consociationibus biblicis...* (*EB* §626).

xxxvi. Ibid. (*EB* §622–33).

xxxvii. 2 Tim 3:15–17.

4

HISTORICAL CRITICISM: ITS ROLE IN BIBLICAL INTERPRETATION AND CHURCH LIFE

Though widely used by Catholic, Jewish, and Protestant interpreters of the Bible, the historical-critical method of interpretation has
come under fire in recent years.[1] Complaints against it have been
voiced, and there is need to see whether they are justified or not.

For instance, integrists in the American Catholic Church have
labeled it Modernist or Neo-Modernist, because they have seen it as
emphasizing the human elements in the Bible and not paying sufficient attention to the Bible as "the Word of God." Attacks on Catholic
biblical scholars who have made use of this method have appeared in
the *Wanderer, U.S. National Catholic Register,* and *Catholicism in
Crisis.*[2] Such integrists have never been able to accept the modern
Catholic interpretation of the Bible and would have all return to the
precritical mode of exposition in vogue in the Church at least since
the sixteenth century.

Complaints also came from the left in individuals such as
Thomas Sheehan, professor of philosophy at Loyola University of
Chicago, who was hailed as "someone with impeccably 'liberal' cre-
dentials…writing in…an impeccably liberal secular publication," the
New York Review of Books.[3] In an article entitled "Revolution in the
Church,"[4] Sheehan claimed that practitioners of the historical-critical
method had become a "liberal consensus," which is "bringing the
Church to what can be called the end of Catholicism." This liberal
consensus was identified with the conclusions proposed by "Catholic
scholars" such as Benoit, Brown, Fitzmyer, Meier, Murphy, Pesch,
and Stanley — and such theologians as Kasper, Küng, Schillebeeckx,
and Tracy, who had made use of the biblical scholars' work. Sheehan
acknowledged that the consensus was the "most vigorous intellectual

59

renaissance since the high Middle Ages," being promoted by exegetes and theologians finally "awakened from a long hibernation." Having adopted advanced techniques from mainly Protestant scholars, they used them for "a radical rethinking of the faith" and "have been dismantling traditional Roman Catholic theology." Their work has brought them to conclusions that "conflict with traditional Catholic doctrines," for they have been raising doubts about the divinity of Christ, the virgin birth, the resurrection of Christ, the infancy narratives, and the Gospel accounts of the claims Jesus supposedly made. Actually, Sheehan's article was a "mixed bag," a "breathless paean to the winning side" (R. McInerny), i.e., the liberal consensus, but also a recognition that the consensus stood in opposition to the "folk religion of most practicing Catholics," which was still living on the pre-revolutionary fare generally served up from local pulpits — "and especially from the one currently occupied by the conservative Pope John Paul II."[5]

Complaints about the historical-critical method of interpretation also came from other quarters more difficult to label. Such complaints castigated the method for being overly preoccupied with the prehistory of the text, and consequently neglecting its final form, its literary features, its canonical setting, and especially the religious or theological meaning of the sacred text.

Related to the third type of complaint was that coming from fundamentalists. In this case, insistence on the inspiration of the biblical text or on the authority of the written Word of God was accompanied by a literalist reading of the Bible to guarantee the fundamentals of Christian doctrine. It became a refusal to analyze the text or to confront its problematic aspects. Problems were not admitted; harmonization of texts was pursued.

Complaints of this sort made many people think that the historical-critical method of interpretation of the Bible had had its day. But has it? Having been trained in this method and having used it widely, with some success, I should now like to answer that question. My further remarks will be made under four headings: (1) origin and development of the method; (2) a description of the method; (3) presuppositions with which it is used; and (4) its role in biblical interpretation and in the life of the Church.

1. Origin and Development of the Method

It is not often recognized that the beginnings of the historical-critical method of interpretation can be traced to the work of the Scholiasts who commented on Greek epic and lyric poets in the library of ancient Alexandria in the last two or three centuries B.C. A good representative of such Scholiasts was Zenodotus of Ephesus, who became the director of the library about 284 B.C. and who collated manuscripts of Homer's writings and compiled a *Homeric Glossary*, a study of difficult words in those writings.

Church writers in the patristic period imitated the techniques developed in such Alexandrian classical philology. Some writers in that period were noted for their forms of criticism, which were perhaps somewhat primitive, if judged by today's standards, but which nevertheless developed into the historical-critical method used in modern times. Thus, Origen's critical work on the Hebrew and Greek texts of the OT resulted in his famous *Hexapla* (or sixfold Bible), which arranged the text in six parallel columns: the Hebrew consonantal text in Hebrew characters; the same Hebrew text in Greek characters to fix the vocalization and proper pronunciation (e.g., ἰαβέ, as the proper pronunciation of Hebrew יהוה, hence "Yahweh"); the Greek version of Aquila; the Greek version of Symmachus; the Greek version of the Septuagint; and the Greek version of Theodotion.[6] Other patristic writers, such as Augustine and Jerome, likewise used critical methods in their commentaries on biblical books.[7] It is necessary to stress this, because most of the patristic commentators did not seek to expound the literal meaning of the biblical text, but allegorized it, being preoccupied with what has been called the "spiritual" sense of Scripture.[8]

The next serious development in the historical-critical method came at the time of the Renaissance, especially in the work of scholars who espoused "getting back to the sources" *(recursus ad fontes)*. Part of that work entailed the study of the Bible in its original languages, Hebrew, Aramaic, and Greek, instead of Latin, as was customary in practically all earlier periods in the Western Church. About that time too, the Copernican revolution likewise had a bearing on the study of the Bible, especially in its aftermath, the Galileo affair. For it affected the interpretation of Josh 10:12–13, which spoke about the sun standing still for a whole day (at a time when people commonly believed that the sun moved around the earth).

Though the Reformers, especially Luther and Calvin, did not radically depart from the traditional interpretation of Scripture, they accorded the Bible a primacy over the Church and its interpretation of Scripture, which gradually resulted in the abandonment of allegorical interpretation and in an emphasis on the literal sense of the original texts.[9]

In the seventeenth and eighteenth centuries, the method was developed further in the work of the Dutch jurist and theologian Hugo Grotius, the French Oratorian and biblical scholar Richard Simon, and the Dutch philosopher Baruch Spinoza — thus in the work of a Protestant, a Catholic, and a Jew.

New impetus was given to the method at the time of the so-called Enlightenment and by the movement of German historicism in the nineteenth century. There was, on the one hand, the influence of Leopold von Ranke, who as a historian sought to present the past *wie es eigentlich gewesen,* "how it really was."[10] That ambitious goal of "objective historiography" affected many biblical scholars of the time. On the other hand, there were the deist attacks on historical Christianity, which also developed the method in various ways. The eighteenth-century deist Hermann Samuel Reimarus had already penned such an attack, but fear of consequences that might ensue deterred him from publishing it during his lifetime. Seven parts of his study were published subsequently by Gottfried Ephraim Lessing under the title *Wolfenbüttel Fragmente* (1774–78).[11] Reimarus's work led eventually to the so-called Life of Jesus research *(Leben-Jesu Forschung)* of the mid-nineteenth century. Then scholars such as Ferdinand Christian Baur, Heinrich E. G. Paulus, David Friedrich Strauss, Bruno Bauer, and Ernest Renan composed their studies of the historical Jesus of Nazareth, treating the Gospels merely as ancient human records.

It is difficult for us today to grasp the impact that the historical and archaeological discoveries of the late eighteenth and early nineteenth centuries had on the development of the historical-critical method of interpretation of ancient texts, but those discoveries were of major importance in that development.[12] Such discoveries could not help but influence biblical interpretation.

The great founder of the Dominican École Biblique in Jerusalem, Marie-Joseph Lagrange, O.P., published in 1904 a small book, *La méthode historique*, which clearly showed that the historical-critical method could be used well by orthodox Catholic interpreters of the Bible.[13] Though Lagrange suffered greatly from the integrists of his day, his contribution to the debate is recalled now with gratitude. The dark cloud of reaction that set in thereafter, especially during the period of Modernism, was lifted finally, when Pope Pius XII issued his encyclical *Divino afflante Spiritu* in 1943.[14]

During the course of the twentieth century, the method was developed further with the refinements of source criticism, form criticism, and redaction criticism. Other historical and archaeological discoveries, especially in Syria and Palestine, shed further light on biblical texts. It is again difficult to comprehend the impact of further discoveries in that century on the historical study of the Bible, but the decipherment of the Ugaritic language in 1929 and the discovery of the Dead Sea Scrolls near Qumran in 1947–56 contributed greatly to the development of the method. So much, then, for the origin and development of the historical-critical method of biblical interpretation.

2. Description of the Method

The method is called "historical-critical," because, as we have seen, it applies to the Bible the critical techniques developed from Alexandrian classical philology.[15] It recognizes that the Bible, though containing the Word of God, is an ancient record, composed by a multitude of authors over a long period of time. Being an ancient composition, it has to be studied and analyzed as are other ancient historical records. Since much of the Bible presents a narrative account of events that affected the lives of ancient Jews and early Christians, the various accounts have to be analyzed against their proper human and historical backgrounds, in their contemporary contexts, and in their original languages. It is called "critical," not because it seeks to criticize the ancient records in any pejorative sense, but because it uses the techniques of different forms of literary and historical criticism.

The method makes use of two preliminary steps, borrowed from classical philology: (1) the consideration of *introductory questions* concerning (a) the authenticity of the writing (e.g., Did Paul write the Epistle to the Ephesians?); (b) the integrity or unity of the writing (Did Paul write all of it, or has the text suffered secondary interpolation?); (c) the date and place of composition; (d) the content of the writing, analyzed according to its structure or outline, its style, and its literary form (Is it a letter, a parable, a prayer? Is it poetry, rhetoric, historical narrative, or fiction?); (e) the occasion and purpose of the writing (i.e., the author's intention in composing it); and (f) its background (Has the OT author been influenced by Assyrian, Babylonian, Egyptian, or Canaanite ideas? Has the NT writer been influenced by Palestinian Jewish, Hellenistic, or eastern Mediterranean ideas?). All such preliminary questions help much in the comprehension of the biblical writings as something coming to us from a definite literary context, time, and place in antiquity.

Likewise borrowed from classical philology is (2) *textual criticism*, which is concerned with the transmission of the biblical text in the original language and in its ancient versions. In what manuscripts does one find the best form of the transmitted text? What are the best families of manuscripts? Do any of the ancient versions contain readings that attest to a text superior to the Greek or Hebrew text that we have inherited? This is a complicated and technical aspect of critical interpretation of the Bible, yet it is clearly fundamental, even though preliminary.

Along with such preliminary questions to which the biblical text is submitted, there are refinements of historical criticism that have come to be associated with it. Though they are not per se historical criticism, they are forms of criticism that in the long run affect the historical judgment about an ancient text.

(1) *Literary criticism* is concerned with the literary and stylistic character and content of the text. Part of such criticism has already been mentioned under the introductory questions listed above (d). In fact, this sort of criticism has long been associated with historical criticism, though some modern literary critics of the Bible often give the impression that such study of it has been overlooked, whereas it is, in their opinion, really superior to historical criticism and of greater importance.[16] It is important, indeed, because it curbs the historical judgment about a text. When one realizes that the ancient author has written poetry (and poetry of a definite kind), or has employed rhetorical

devices (*inclusio,* chiasmus, catchword bonds), or has argued in a definite way (from cause to effect, from effect to cause), one then realizes that the historical aspect of his writing may not be his primary concern.

(2) Another refinement of historical criticism has been *source criticism*, which seeks to determine the prehistory of a biblical text. What sources did the biblical writer use in composing his text? In some biblical books, the text simply cries out for such source analysis because of parallel accounts of the same event, stereotyped phraseology, etc. If the book forms part of the Pentateuch, the interpreter has to discern the difference of composition among the Yahwist, Elohist, Deuteronomic, and Priestly writings. If the text is part of a Synoptic Gospel, the distinction of it as derived from Mark, or "Q," or from private Matthean or Lucan sources is an important aspect of the interpretation of the passage. Source criticism is not an end in itself, and the interpreter's task is far from finished once the source of the passage has been determined. But the difference in the parallels, analyzed as derived from different sources, often affects the historical judgment about a text and aids in the final understanding of it.

(3) A third refinement of historical criticism is *form criticism.* Applied first of all to the OT by H. Gunkel, it was used to interpret the Synoptic Gospels in the work of M. Dibelius and R. Bultmann in the early part of the twentieth century. It seeks to determine the literary form or subform of a given biblical writing. What kind of a psalm is it? Is the text part of apocalyptic or Wisdom literature? Is it a parable or other type of saying of Jesus, a miracle story, a pronouncement story? These forms are diverse, and one learns from form criticism to switch mental gears in reading biblical passages. But one also learns much about the history of the form and how it has developed in the tradition. Such form-critical analysis of biblical passages certainly affects one's historical judgment about them. Moreover, from such analysis one has learned that the truth of the passage is analogous to its form.[17] And therein lies the crucial relationship of form criticism to historical criticism.

(4) *Redaction criticism* is a further refinement of historical criticism, because it seeks to determine how certain biblical writers, using traditional materials, have modified, edited, or redacted the sources of whatever they may have inherited from writers or communities before them in the interest of their own literary goal or purpose. Such redac-

tion is often evident in the language and style of a given biblical writer. Once such redaction is discerned, it too has a bearing on the historical judgment of a passage.

Finally, it should be clear that the use of all such criticism is geared to one end: to determine the meaning of the text as it was intended and expressed by the human author moved long ago to compose it. Since the truth that he has enshrined in his text is analogous to the form used, historical criticism teaches us that we cannot read an ancient text without the sophistication that the form calls for.

Furthermore, we have learned through this method that not everything narrated in the past tense necessarily corresponds to ancient reality, and that not everything put on the lips of Jesus of Nazareth by evangelists was necessarily so uttered by him. In regard to the historical criticism of the Synoptic Gospels, we have learned through this method to distinguish three stages of the gospel tradition: (I) what Jesus of Nazareth did and said (corresponding roughly to A.D. 1–33); (II) what apostles of Jesus preached about him, his words, and his deeds (corresponding roughly to A.D. 33–65); and (III) what evangelists wrote about him, having culled, synthesized, and explicated the tradition that preceded them, each in his own way (corresponding to A.D. 65–95).[18] The relationship of Stage III to Stages I and II is *the* problem for modern readers of these Gospels, and therein lies the crucial need of the historical-critical method of Gospel interpretation.[19]

3. Presuppositions with Which the Method Is Used

One reason why the historical-critical method of biblical interpretation has fallen under suspicion recently is that it was tainted at an important stage in its development with presuppositions that are not necessarily part of it. Thus, it was tainted seriously by the rationalist presuppositions with which the *Leben-Jesu Forschung* once used it. The *Wolfenbüttel Fragmente* of Reimarus and the lives of Jesus composed by Baur, Strauss, Renan, and others stemmed either from deist attacks on historical Christianity or historical studies that sought to be liberated from all dogmatic influence, so that the Gospels could be analyzed solely as records of antiquity. Adolf von Harnack, the patrologist and church historian, sought to curb the extreme tendencies of

that allegedly presuppositionless study of the historical Jesus, and emphasized a respect for tradition; but he never abandoned the historical-
critical method itself. It remained for Albert Schweitzer to unmask the
efforts of the Life-of-Jesus research. In his famous book, *The Quest of
the Historical Jesus*, Schweitzer showed that such investigation of the
life of Jesus had sprung not from a purely historical interest in Jesus
but from a "struggle against the tyranny of dogma," and that the greatest of such "lives" of Jesus, those by Reimarus and Strauss, had been
"written with hate" — "not so much hate of the Person of Jesus as of
the supernatural nimbus with which it was so easy to surround him."[20]
The rationalist attacks on traditional Christianity, especially in its
supernatural aspects, were linked to an otherwise neutral method and
tainted it unduly. What was at fault was the presupposition with which
the method was used, and not the method itself.

At a still later date, the historical-critical method was employed
again by K. L. Schmidt, M. Dibelius, and R. Bultmann in their work
on NT form criticism. Bultmann's contribution proved to be the most
influential; yet he too associated the method with presuppositions. He
linked historical criticism with a form of kerygmatic theology that
depended heavily on Luther's teaching about justification by faith
alone, D. F. Strauss's mythical interpretation of the Gospels, and M.
Heidegger's existentialist philosophy. Emphasis on the preached Word
and justification *sola fide* resulted in Bultmann's lack of interest in the
Jesus of history himself, or what the Jesus of Stage I of the gospel tradition did or said in Nazareth, Capernaum, or Jerusalem. Bultmann
was interested solely in what the gospel proclaims and how its
preached Word affects the individual believer of today. He sought thus
to subordinate event to word; indeed, for him the word may be said to
generate the event. Hence Bultmann's lengthy treatment of the form
he called an "apophthegm,"[21] and his unconcern about the lack of
continuity between Stage II of the gospel tradition and Stage I. The
event narrated was unimportant so long as the reader was accosted by
the apophthegm or punch-line enshrined in it. Thus Bultmann was
led to the demythologization of the event. For the quest of the historical basis of the kerygma was for him a betrayal of the principle of faith
alone. Rather, NT theology began with the primitive kerygma — and
not before it.[22] The kerygma addresses us through the NT, and its
Word is the basis as well as the object of our faith. Moreover, that

preached Word has to be understood in a Heideggerian existentialist fashion, as it elicits from us a "yes," the affirmation of one's personal authentic existence. In reality, this authentic existence is a gift of God that comes from the opening of one's self to the grace of forgiveness announced in the kerygma.[23]

Despite the laudable pastoral thrust of Bultmann's concern to make the NT message a challenge for people in the mid-twentieth century, he thus associated the historical-critical method with philosophical and theological presuppositions that proved to be not universally acceptable.[24]

The foregoing paragraphs reveal two examples of presuppositions with which the historical-critical method was used in the past: the rationalist, antidogmatic presupposition; and the demythologizing, existentialist presupposition. To these two, one could easily add the presuppositions of the so-called Jesus Seminar in the late twentieth century, which shared many of the same concerns as the first-mentioned of the two preceding ones.[25]

The irony of the matter is that Bultmann himself once queried whether presuppositionless interpretation were ever possible.[26]

Modern Christian interpreters of the Bible also use the historical-critical method with presuppositions — but presuppositions of a different sort. To explain such presuppositions, let me first say a word about "exegesis," a term by which the interpretation of Scripture according to this method is often known. The Greek noun *exēgēsis* is derived from the verb *exēgeomai*, "draw out." The aim of "exegesis" is to draw out from a text the meaning of its words, phrases, and paragraphs. *Webster's Third International Dictionary* defines exegesis as a "critical interpretation of a text or a portion of Scripture." Thus, English and some other modern languages have this special term for such a critical interpretation of Scripture. For exegesis, though it uses the philological tools and techniques, differs from philology, because it is *philology plus*. And the plus is the presupposition with which one employs this critical method.

Exegesis is concerned in the long run with the sense of a biblical passage in its final form: it seeks to draw out the meaning of the passage intended by the inspired writer. This includes not only the *textual meaning* (the sense of its words and phrases), but also its *contextual meaning* (their sense in a given paragraph or episode), and its *relational meaning* (their sense is relation to the book or corpus of writings as a whole). The relational meaning is called at times its biblical-theological meaning, because it seeks to interpret the words and phrases according to the synthesis of ideas of the biblical writer. The combination of the textual, contextual, and relational meanings of a passage leads to the discovery of its religious and theological meaning — to its meaning as the Word of God couched in ancient human language.

Herein lies the plus or the presupposition with which a modern Christian interpreter of the Bible employs the philological tools and techniques characteristic of the historical-critical method. For the plus consists of elements of faith or belief: that the text being critically interpreted contains God's Word set forth in human words of long ago; that it has been composed under the guidance of the Spirit and has authority for the people of the Jewish-Christian heritage; that it is part of a restricted collection of authoritative writings (part of a canon); that it has been given by God for the edification and salvation of his people; and that it is properly expounded only in relation to the Tradition that has grown out of it within the communal faith-life of that people.

Since the historical-critical method is per se neutral, it can be used with such faith presuppositions. Indeed, by reason of them it becomes a *properly oriented* method of biblical interpretation, for none of the elements of the method is pursued in and for itself. They are used only to achieve the main goal of ascertaining what the biblical message was that the sacred writer of old sought to convey — in effect, the literal sense of the Bible.

Because the method is neutral, it can still undergo refinements in either its historical or literary features. New approaches to interpretation are proposed from time to time, and some of them serve to correct the basic method (such as rhetorical criticism, narrative criticism, canonical criticism, etc.); but none of them is a substitute for the fundamental method, and none can be allowed to replace it.

4. The Role of the Method in Biblical Interpretation and the Life of the Church

The use of historical criticism in the interpretation of the Bible is not a temporary fad, because it has been advocated by the highest authority in the Catholic Church. In his encyclical *Divino afflante Spiritu*, Pope Pius XII never uses the term "historical criticism," yet his recommendations for the definitive understanding of the Bible clearly follow the principles of the method.[27] For Pius XII insisted on (1) the study of the Bible in its original languages; (2) the interpretation of it according to the ancient literary forms or genres; and (3) the application to the biblical text of modern discoveries, "whether in the domain of archaeology or ancient history or literature,...as well as their manner and art of reasoning, narrating, and writing."[28] That insistence of Pius XII freed Roman Catholic biblical interpretation from its own form of fundamentalism, inherited from the post-Tridentine era and the Counter-Reformation. Pius XII did, indeed, emphasize the need to spell out the literal meaning of the sacred text, but with due regard for the literary form in which it was composed.[29]

Pius XII, however, did not stop with insistence on the need to ascertain the literal sense of a biblical text, for he saw it clearly as related to the "theological doctrine in faith and morals of the individual books or texts."[30] Such a theological exposition of Scripture would reduce to silence those who claim that "they scarcely ever find anything in biblical commentaries to raise their hearts to God, to nourish their souls or promote their interior life."[31] This is precisely what the properly oriented use of the historical-critical method can and does achieve in the interpretation of the Bible and the life of the Church.

The recommendation of this method did not die with Pius XII, because in 1964 the Biblical Commission issued an Instruction, *On the Historical Truth of the Gospels*, which did not merely affirm again the historicity of the Gospels but proved to be a nuanced, enlightened discussion of the stages of the gospel tradition that I have already mentioned.[32] For the Commission insisted:

> Unless the exegete pays attention to all these things [the three stages of the gospel tradition], which pertain to the origin and composition of the Gospels, and makes proper use of all the laudable achievements of recent research, he will not fulfill his task of probing into what the sacred writers intended and what they really said. (par. X)

Among the "laudable achievements" singled out were the "reasonable elements" of the form-critical method, which it mentioned explicitly by name (par. V). Thus the method itself, which was derived from non-Catholic interpreters of the Bible, received a clear approbation, but not the presuppositions with which it had sometimes been used by them. Moreover, the substance of the Instruction was taken up and adopted by the Fathers of the Second Vatican Council in the Dogmatic Constitution on Revelation, *Dei Verbum*.[33]

Furthermore, in 1984 the Biblical Commission issued another document, *Bible et christologie*.[34] It discusses eleven different approaches to Christology in modern times and points out the risks that each one runs; then it gives an overview of the biblical testimony to Jesus the Christ. It is a lengthy document that names names, mentioning scholars who are representatives of the various approaches: from traditional manual Christology based on the Councils of Nicaea and Chalcedon and medieval scholastic theologians to such modern theologians as Rahner, Schillebeeckx, and Küng. What is striking in the document is the number of obiter dicta scattered throughout it, which call for a critical reading of the OT and NT. Nowhere in the document does the Commission speak of the historical-critical method, but in its effort to present an overview of "integral Christology" (the total testimony of the Bible to Jesus Christ) it insists time and again on "the demands of biblical criticism" (e.g., in 1.2.7.2), which it clearly distinguishes from "critical hypotheses…always subject to revision" (1.2.10). One paragraph of the document is worth quoting:

> Indeed, many problems still remain obscure about the composition process of the sacred writings that finally emerged from their inspired authors. As a result, those who would dispense with the study of problems of this sort would be approaching Scripture only in a superficial way; wrongly judging that their way of reading Scripture is "theological," they would be setting off on a deceptive route. Solutions that are too easy can in no way provide the solid basis needed for studies in biblical theology, even when engaged in with full faith. (1.3.3)

What ultimately lies behind this critical approach to the study of the Bible in the Church is the conviction that God's revelation in Christ took place in the past, and the ancient record of that self-manifestation of God in him is disclosed to the Church above all in the Bible, in the Word of God couched in ancient human wording. This is the fundamental reason why historical criticism of it plays an important role in the life of the Church itself. This admission does not want to deny the guidance and assistance of the Spirit in Church life. Yet that Spirit is never conceived of as a revealer. The Spirit guides the Church through the centuries into a fuller and deeper understanding of the historical revelation once given in Christ Jesus. As the Fourth Evangelist put it, "The Paraclete, the holy Spirit, whom the Father will send in my name, will teach you all things and will remind you of all that I have said to you" (14:26); and "when the Spirit of Truth comes, he will guide you into all truth, for he will not speak on his own authority" (16:13). Thus historical criticism assists the Church in its ongoing life, by helping it to uncover the essence of the revelation once given to it — the meaning of the Word of God in ancient human words.[35]

Modern literary critics insist sometimes that a text once composed takes on a life of its own and may even convey a meaning beyond that of the original author's intention. There is some truth in that view, especially when it is a question of poetry, but such a "meaning" that goes "beyond" that of the historical biblical author can never be understood as losing all homogeneity with the original meaning of the author. However, such a meaning that goes "beyond" the original biblical meaning may become part of the Spirit-guided postwritten status of the text, viz., that which has become its genuine dogmatic Tradition. Such a defense of the historical-critical method of interpreting the Bible may seem as though I am imposing a heavy burden on readers, who might justly object: "Why does one have to know all these things about the Bible? Why cannot one just open the book and read it — read it as the Word of God?" Such a question is often asked. The answer to it comes from two passages in the Bible itself. The first is found in 2 Pet 3:15–17, which reads:

> Consider the forbearance of our Lord as salvation, just as our brother Paul once wrote to you according to the wisdom granted to him, speaking of this in all his letters. Some things

in them are hard to understand, which the unlearned and unstable twist to their own destruction, as they do the other Scriptures. Knowing this in advance, beloved [Christians], be on your guard that you be not carried away by the error of lawless people and fall from your surefootedness.

Whoever wrote that passage at the beginning of the second Christian century was already aware of the difficulty that people were having with the proper understanding of Paul's letters.

The second passage is even more eloquent. It is found in the Acts of the Apostles, where Philip the Evangelist, who has been preaching the word of God in Samaria, is told by the angel of the Lord to go down the road from Jerusalem to Gaza. He does so and encounters the eunuch of the Ethiopian Candace seated in his chariot and reading Isaiah 53, as he returns to his land from a visit to Jerusalem. Philip draws near and asks him whether he understands what he is reading. The Ethiopian's answer is well known: "How can I, unless someone guides me?" (8:31). Thus the soon-to-be-baptized Ethiopian Jew reveals his difficult experience in trying to understand a passage about the Servant of the Lord in the Book of Isaiah — an experience that is often that of the modern reader of the Bible as well. Yet it is also the experience with which the historical-critical method of interpreting the Bible is trying to cope: to guide the reader.

Finally, there is an aspect of the historical-critical interpretation of the Bible in the life of the Church that has to be mentioned, at least briefly, viz., its impact in ecumenical relations with other Christian Churches. The use of this method by Catholic interpreters since 1943 had much to do with the preparation of the Church for the developments at the Second Vatican Council. On the heels of that Council emerged the ecumenical dialogue with many Christian ecclesial communities. No little reason for that emergence was precisely the fact that Catholic interpreters of the Bible were using the same kind of interpretation of the Bible that was current among many non-Catholic interpreters. That was not a direct consequence of historical criticism of the Bible, but it was an aspect of it that should not be overlooked.[36] Would the varied bilateral consultations be where they are today, if it were not for the use of the historical-critical method of biblical interpretation in the Catholic Church?

5

CONCERNING THE INTERPRETATION
OF THE BIBLE IN THE CHURCH

A British scholar named Philip R. Davies, professor in the department of biblical studies at the University of Sheffield, published a small book in 1995 entitled *Whose Bible Is It Anyway?*[1] Although Davies says that he enjoys "biblical scholarship,"[2] he prefers to evaluate biblical writings "from a disinterested perspective," such as a "critical observer" might apply to other literature.[3] He asks, "Do religious writings make any sense to any reader who does not accept the reality of the deities they refer to?" and "Do those who claim a religious affinity with a certain body of writings have a better instinct for the meaning of those writings?"[4] Davies seeks rigorously to distinguish a confessional approach to the Bible from a nonconfessional approach. For him both approaches may claim to be critical, but they are "so fundamentally divergent" as "to imply separate disciplines."[5] As exemplars of such nonconfessional interpretation, Davies names Dante, Blake, and Eliot. He further insists that there is no realistic hope of imposing an ecclesial interpretation on readers "outside the ecclesial domain," because such a domain "cannot claim jurisdiction over how bibles are to be defined and read outside its own bounds."[6]

For Davies there is in reality no Bible, only "bibles" recognized by different communities, and the phrase "biblical text" means no more than a text found in some bible. Hence for him, the adjective "biblical" imparts no essence or characteristic to a given text than that, viz., it is found in some bible. Moreover, there is for Davies no such thing as a "biblical writer." "No bible ever had an author or writer." "There is nothing in the term 'biblical' that tells us anything useful about the author, except that his or her work was taken up later into someone's canon."[7]

So argues Davies in defense of his "nonconfessional scholarship." He characterizes his stance toward the Bible as "humanist" and "agnostic about deities."[8] Although he insists that he does not write "because of some atheist prejudice," he claims that in chapters 4, 5, and 7 of his book "the deity is treated...as a character in a story *because that is how the writers of these texts wanted it to be.*"[9]

> Whether their private beliefs about deities corresponded exactly to what they wrote depends on whether or not we treat them seriously as creative writers. I see no reason to insist that biblical storytellers, any more than modern ones, feel obliged to write only what they themselves hold to be true.[10]

Nevertheless, Davies maintains that his stance does not "diminish one's joy in reading a bible."[11]

I cite these views of Davies mainly because of the title of his book, *Whose Bible Is It Anyway?* and because they reveal a mode of interpreting the Bible that is different from what I am discussing in this book. Although Davies says he recognizes a confessional approach, he is nevertheless more concerned to advance "nonconfessional scholarship," and that is the purpose of his book.

The answer to Davies' question for the normal Christian would be, "The Church's Bible," [12] because the Bible belongs to the Christian Church, Catholic, Orthodox, or Protestant.[13] The obvious reason for saying this is that there was no "Bible" before a faith-community decided what writings passed on an authoritative message to its constituent members and to successive generations of them. Or, to put it as a NT writer has phrased it, there was no Bible before a faith-community decided which writings were "divinely inspired and profitable for teaching, for reproof, for correction, and for training in uprightness" (2 Tim 3:16).

The process of deciding about authoritative writings began long before the NT. In ancient Israel, Jews of old recognized which books authoritatively transmitted their religious outlook on life and best reflected their relations with Yahweh or Elohim. Long before the NT teaching about the inspiration of "all Scripture," Jews recognized the authority of "Moses and the Prophets," i.e., of the Pentateuch and of the Former and Latter Prophets.[14] This is made clear in the Dead Sea Scrolls from pre-Christian Jewish Palestine. There God issues commands to the Qumran Jewish community "through Moses and through all his servants the Prophets."[15] It is likewise clear from the NT, which picks up from that Palestinian Judaism the authoritative phrase, "Moses and the Prophets" (Luke 16:29, 31; 24:27; Acts 28:23).

That means that before Israel of old decided which writings were authoritative for it, no Jewish writer ever composed a book in order that it might become a "biblical" or "canonical" text. In this regard, I agree with Davies. The prophetic oracles of Isaiah, Jeremiah, or Ezekiel were not compiled in order to become part of the Jewish canon of Scripture. Those oracles, even inspired by God, were uttered by God's mouthpieces to direct and guide Israel in its relation to Yahweh in varied circumstances. They were written down only subsequently to preserve those directives for generations in Israel to come. In such a written form, they gradually acquired authoritative status for subsequent generations of Jews, which, as a faith-community, acknowledged their value. That process of recognition and acknowledgment was continued later among early Christians, who not only adopted the Hebrew Scriptures of the Jews as the OT, but added to them their own authoritative writings, viz., the NT. It was the Christian faith-community that accepted *some* Christian writings into its collection and not others. For this reason, one sees why the Bible is the Church's book: It is the collection of authoritative ancient writings that the faith-community of early Christians has passed on to subsequent generations, and even to Christians of today.

Such an answer, however, to the question posed by Davies is a confessional answer. It is not the answer that he, as a humanist or an agnostic, would like to hear; but if it were not for such subsequent acts of recognition and acknowledgment by Jewish and Christian faith-communities, there would be no Bible for "nonconfessional scholarship" to study. Even though the Bible may rightly belong to world literature and may be esteemed by humanists and agnostics as well as by committed Jews and Christians, it is not so esteemed or classified merely because of its humanist or literary merits.[16] It has been given that status, because it has been recognized as the written Word of God, who is not just a "character" in the narrative tales of the "biblical storytellers." The authors of the texts that make up the OT not only regarded Yahweh or Elohim as their God, but also sought to get others so to acknowledge him. Moreover, Paul of Tarsus summed up the

Christian attitude, when he wrote, "For us there is one God, the Father, from whom come all things and toward whom we tend; and there is one Lord, Jesus Christ, through whom all things come and through whom we are destined" (1 Cor 8:6).

Such an answer to Davies' question gives rise to another: How, then, does one interpret the Bible in the Christian faith community? An important answer to the latter question has been given in the document of the Biblical Commission issued in 1993, *The Interpretation of the Bible in the Church*. My further remarks will be a summary of that document, along with comments on some of the problems that it has raised.[17] These remarks will be made under four headings: (1) the historical-critical method of interpreting Scripture; (2) other approaches to Scripture; (3) the senses of Scripture; and (4) the actualization of the literal sense of Scripture.

1. The Historical-Critical Method of Interpreting Scripture

It is somewhat ironic that, at a time when one was hearing complaints about the historical-critical method of biblical interpretation and repeated calls for other methods to replace it, the Biblical Commission devoted a considerable portion of its 1993 document to that mode of interpretation, precisely to put it in a proper perspective. Although the Commission acknowledged that the method had not always been used properly and had been judged "deficient from the point of view of faith,"[18] it still regarded it as

> the indispensable method for the scientific study of the meaning of ancient texts. Holy Scripture, inasmuch as it is the "Word of God in human language," has been composed by human authors in all its various parts and in all the sources that lie behind them. Because of this, its proper understanding not only admits the use of this method, but actually requires it.[19]

In saying this, the Commission recognized, in effect, that the Bible was composed during the course of a millennium and comes to us today from an ancient period more than two thousand years ago. It was not written in twentieth-century English, but rather in Hebrew, Greek, and Aramaic by human beings of diverse cultures in the ancient eastern Mediterranean world. That is why the adjective "historical" is so important in the name of this method, which is particularly attentive to the ancient meaning of the biblical text and its underlying sources and traditions.

Although people sometimes say that the historical-critical method came into use at the time of the Enlightenment, it is actually far older. The Commission rightly recognized that "certain elements" of it "are very ancient."

> They were used in antiquity by Greek commentators of classical literature and, much later, in the course of the Patristic period, by authors such as Origen, Jerome, and Augustine. The method at that time was much less developed. Its modern forms are the result of refinements brought about especially since the time of the Renaissance humanists and their *recursus ad fontes* (return to the sources).[20]

The historical-critical method, when used in biblical interpretation, has as its goal the ascertaining of the literal sense of the written Word of God. For a description of the method, see chapter 4.

Sometimes Catholics who are impatient with the historical-critical method ask, "Why should not modern biblical scholars interpret the Bible as did the Fathers of the Church or other writers of the patristic period?" The main reason is that so much has happened in this world since the patristic period. The Catholic Church, in its interpretation of Scripture, has learned much from the scholars of the Renaissance and the Reformation. The Renaissance emphasis on *recursus ad fontes* opened up the study of the Bible to its original languages and some of its ancient versions, which notably changed the orientation and interpretation of the whole Western Church, which previously had read the Bible only in the Latin language, either the Vulgate or the *Vetus Latina*. That new study in the Renaissance period opened, indeed, the way further to the translation of the Bible into various vernaculars among the Reformers. It also broke with the highly allegorical, typological, and homiletic interpretation that had characterized the patristic and early medieval modes of expounding the biblical text, which in many cavalier ways disregarded the contexts and the basic literal meaning of the Mosaic, prophetic, and sapiential writings of the OT.

The Catholic Church also learned much from scholars at the time of the so-called Enlightenment, even though it resisted their rationalistic and anti-dogmatic presuppositions. Today we often forget how, on the heels of the Enlightenment, great historical and archaeological discoveries of the nineteenth century affected our reading of the Bible. Such discoveries were unexpected, but they made it impossible for one to interpret the Bible in the simplistic and often allegorical ways that had been in vogue since the time of the Fathers of the Church and of medieval theologians.

For instance, the well-known Rosetta Stone, inscribed in 196 B.C. to honor King Ptolemy V Epiphanes for many benefactions he had made to Egyptian temples, was written in hieroglyphic Egyptian, Demotic, and Greek. The stone was discovered in the western part of the Nile Delta in 1798 during a Napoleonic expedition there. Its Greek text was read easily, but its chief hieroglyphic text and the Demotic text remained unread, until the former of these texts was deciphered in 1821–22 by the Frenchman Jean François Champollion. The decipherment of Egyptian hieroglyphs was perfected only with the work of the German scholar Karl Richard Lepsius, on the Decree of Canopus in 1866.[21] Then, in the last third of the nineteenth century, one began to read for the first time the literature of ancient Egyptians, i.e., the literature of Israel's neighbors to the west.[22] Then, too, for the first time one was able to compare biblical texts with parallel literary genres. The historical, hymnic, ritual, mythical, and sapiential writings of ancient Egypt thus provided important parallels and counterparts for many similar OT passages.

The same holds true for Assyrian and Babylonian literature. The less-well-known Bisitun Stone[23] stood for many centuries on the caravan road from Ecbatana in Media (northern Iran today) to Babylon (now in Iraq). It still bears a sixth-century B.C. inscription, written in three languages, Old Persian, Elamite, and Babylonian. These different forms of cuneiform record the victory of King Darius I over a rebel, Gaumata, and other of his regal achievements. In 1835, an Englishman, Henry C. Rawlinson, was the first to climb up to the site and copy the inscription. It was deciphered finally in 1839, as a result of the work done by

79

Rawlinson, a German G. F. Grotefend, an Irishman Edward Hincks, and a Frenchman Jules Oppert.[24] That decipherment proved to be the key that unlocked the secret treasures of Assyrian and Babylonian literatures.[25] Then, for the first time, Israel's law codes, historical writings, poetry, didactic, and sapiential texts could be studied in comparison with the literature of its neighbors to the east.

Moreover, in the latter part of the nineteenth century, thousands of Greek papyri were uncovered in Egypt and shed new light on the language of the Septuagint and the NT. These papyrus texts showed that the Greek Bible, on which so much of the Christian tradition had depended for centuries, was written not in "the language of the Holy Ghost," as many had tried to characterize the peculiar form of Greek in which biblical writings had been translated or composed, but in ordinary Hellenistic or Koine Greek current in the last three centuries B.C. and the first century A.D.[26]

In a similar way, one must recall two twentieth-century findings that further influenced biblical interpretation: the first was the discovery in 1929 at ancient Ugarit (modern Ras Shamra in Syria) of hundreds of clay tables inscribed in an alphabetic cuneiform script with a Northwest Semitic language related to Hebrew. The Ugaritic language was deciphered by H. Bauer of Germany and E. Dhorme and C. Virolleaud of France, and it revealed important Canaanite parallels to Hebrew poetry, especially the Psalms.[27] The second was the discovery in 1947–1956 of the Dead Sea Scrolls near Qumran in the British Mandate of Palestine and in the Jordanian-controlled West Bank of what is now part of Israel. They contributed greatly to the interpretation of the OT and to the understanding of the Palestinian Jewish matrix, in which many of the NT writings came into being.[28]

Such discoveries of ancient Egyptian, Assyrian-Babylonian, and Ugaritic literature, of Hellenistic Greek documents, and of the Dead Sea Scrolls have opened up areas of information and comparable religious literature, which were unknown to interpreters of the Bible in the patristic, medieval, Renaissance, or even the Reformation periods. As a result, it became clear how important it was to understand the Bible according to its ancient literary genres or literary forms. These discoveries thus explain why modern biblical interpreters must use the historical-critical method of interpretation and why they cannot be restricted to the allegorical and fanciful exposition that characterized so much of the patristic and medieval understanding of the Bible.

Unfortunately, some of these discoveries aided and abetted also the rationalist interpretation of the Bible inherited from the so-called Enlightenment. They gave rise to the notorious *Babel-Bibel* controversy in German-speaking lands, in which the law codes of Assyria and Babylonia were claimed to be the source of much Mosaic legislation, whereas previous generations of Christians and Jews had regarded it simply as divinely inspired. These discoveries and such use made of them were part of the reason why Pope Leo XIII issued his encyclical *Providentissimus Deus* (1893) to give guidance to Catholic biblical interpreters.[29]

Though Pope Benedict XV, in his encyclical *Spiritus Paraclitus* (1920), could find no good in the study of the literary genres of the Bible,[30] Pope Pius XII corrected that misguided advice in his encyclical *Divino afflante Spiritu* (1943).[31] He insisted not only on the use of the results of the historical and archaeological discoveries of the nineteenth and twentieth centuries, but also on the translation of the Bible from its original languages and the interpretation of it according to the ancient literary genres or forms in which it had been composed. Even though Pius XII never used the name of the historical-critical method, his counsels clearly advocated the use of that method in expounding the literal sense of the Bible.

2. Other Approaches to Scripture

If the Biblical Commission considered the historical-critical method not only "indispensable," but "actually required" for the proper interpretation of Scripture, it also granted that that basic method could be refined and even in some respects corrected by other approaches that have been advocated more recently. Among new methods of literary analysis, the Commission singled out for comment rhetorical analysis, narrative analysis, and semiotic analysis.[32] The first two of these approaches are refinements of the literary criticism of the Bible that was already part of the basic historical-critical method. Their newness is found in the systematic application of these approaches to the interpretation of Scripture. Because much of the

Bible is written to persuade readers to adopt a certain mode of religious life and spirituality, it is not surprising that elements of classical Greek and Roman rhetoric are found in the Bible, along with its Semitic mode of argumentation. Again, because much of the Bible tells stories and recounts events in order to present the history of God's salvific plan and a powerful recital of its liturgy and catechesis, it is not surprising that new forms of narrative analysis help in the proper understanding of the Bible's message. The study of the plot, characters, and system of values of different biblical accounts brings out at times aspects of some passages that have been neglected in the past. The distinction between the "real author" and the "implied reader" have been profitably introduced into the study of some biblical passages.

In addition to such methods of analysis, the Commission also considered a number of approaches to the Bible that have been based on tradition. Among these are the following: (1) The canonical approach, which emphasizes the relation of each biblical text to the Bible as a whole, as a norm for the beliefs espoused by a faith-community. In this way, one can see how the Book of Isaiah would be interpreted with some differences for Jews and Christians, who have different canons. (2) The approach through recourse to Jewish traditions of interpretation. This approach is especially pertinent to the study of the NT, since it seeks to apply to NT writings what can be learned from the Jewish mode of interpretation now found in the writings of the Dead Sea Scrolls, in the targums (interpretative translations of the OT into Aramaic), and in many Jewish parabiblical writings. (3) The approach governed by the history of the text's reception, i.e., the way a given passage has been used in subsequent centuries in theology, literature, asceticism, and mysticism. This approach is called in German *Wirkungsgeschichte*, the "history of the effects," which a given text has had. It is important because it is a way of studying the text in light of the tradition that it has created.

There are also approaches to the Bible that make use of human sciences: (4) the sociological approach; (5) the approach through cultural anthropology; and (6) the psychological approach. Finally, there are also contextual or advocacy approaches: that of (7) liberation theology; and (8) feminism. What must be noted about these newer approaches is that no one of them is valid as a substitute for the historical-critical method itself. They have been, however, and can continue to be, valuable refinements of that basic method, even offering at times useful correctives. In each case, the Commission has evaluated the advantages and disadvantages of the approach.

Before I leave this question of other approaches, I have to mention the fundamentalist reading of the Bible. The Commission is rather critical of Fundamentalism. First, the Commission separated this literalist reading of the Bible from the methods and approaches in which it found value.[33] Second, the basic problem with such a way of reading the Bible is an ideology that is itself not biblical and does not stem from the Bible. It often brings to the reading of the Bible a presupposition of divine dictation and a mode of understanding that prescinds from or fails to cope with the literary genres or forms in which God's Word was formulated by human beings long ago. As Christians, we must be interested in the *literal sense* of God's written Word, but that is something quite different from a literalist reading of it, as if it were dictated by the Holy Spirit.[34]

3. The Senses of Scripture

Earlier I noted that the goal of the properly oriented historical-critical method of interpreting the Bible has been always to ascertain its ancient literal meaning: what the human author sought to express as he passed on God's inspired message to the faith-community. That raises the question about the real meaning of Scripture, or its senses, and the Commission also wanted to provide some guidance in this matter, taking up in turn the literal sense, the spiritual sense, and the fuller sense of Scripture. Each of these senses will be discussed in chapter 6.

4. The Actualization of the Literal Sense of Scripture

What is new in the 1993 document of the Biblical Commission is the emphasis given to the "actualization" of the literal sense of Scripture. As I have said already, the literal sense is the goal of a properly oriented historical-critical interpretation of the Bible. By "properly oriented," I mean the use of that method with the presupposition of Christian faith, that one is interpreting the written Word of God couched in ancient human language, with a message not only for the people of old, but also for Christians of today. As the Fathers of the Second Vatican Council discussed in no little detail,[35] that Word of God "is not a dead word, imprisoned in the past, but a living word, immediately addressed to the man of today."[36]

Although actualization is only an aspect of the literal sense, the Commission has not treated it under the senses of Scripture (it is discussed in part IV, "The Interpretation of the Bible in the Life of the Church").[37] It concerns how one applies the literal sense to the lives of present-day Christians. It may involve the rereading of Scripture "in the light of new circumstances" and the application of it "to the contemporary situation of the People of God."[38] It would be a mistake, however, to think that the Commission has spoken of "the priority of actualization."[39] The Commission did not single out actualization or give it any priority, because actualization is only a building upon the properly ascertained literal sense. It extends it homogeneously to show how what was meant still has meaning for today. Any actualized meaning that does not preserve such a homogeneous connection with what was meant or with the literal sense becomes, in effect, an extraneous sense foisted on the Word of God. It thus becomes eisegesis, the opposite of exegesis, or an accommodated sense (see chapter 6).

When the literal sense of the inspired ancient writings in the Bible is actualized properly, the Word of God speaks to the Christian of today. It produces not merely a renewed interest in the Bible, but a kind of spirituality that is basic to Christian life. All Christian spirituality should be based biblically, founded on the written Word of God, no matter what accidental form it may also take.[40] The basic reason for such spirituality is that the Bible is the Church's book.

Conclusion

In concluding, I may return to the question with which I began, "Whose Bible is it anyway?" The agnostic Davies may think that he has as much right as anyone else to interpret the Bible, a right that we may be willing to concede at first. Nevertheless, even the agnostic nonconfessional interpreter must realize that there would be no Bible for him or her to interpret, were it not for the faith-communities, the people of Israel of old and the early Christians. There would be no "Bible" for such "nonconfessional scholarship."

Moreover, when Davies tries to tell us that the authors of the writings that are found in our differing "bibles" did not seek to get us to reverence Yahweh or Elohim as the God of the Universe, he is simply missing the point of the Bible entirely. He may protest that he has as much of an instinct for the meaning of such writings as those who claim a *religious* affinity with them, but in so protesting he fails to see the pertinence of such writings to his own life. That, in the long run, is why the Biblical Commission, in its document of 1993, put so much insistence on "the Interpretation of the Bible" within the Church.

6

THE SENSES OF SCRIPTURE

The meaning of a passage of Scripture has been a matter of discussion ever since the emergence of the NT. Writers of books in that Testament often quoted passages from the OT, using them in different ways.[1] That interpretation of Scripture became problematic and has often been discussed and debated. Indeed, some of the ways in which NT writers used the OT texts gave rise to similar interpretations by later Christian writers who imitated them. Luke, for instance, at the end of his Gospel records the risen Christ saying, "All that was written about me in the Law of Moses, in the Prophets, and in the Psalms must see fulfillment" (24:44). From that mode of thinking arose the Christian global reading of the OT as *praeparatio evangelica*.[2] A later writer, who depended on the canonical Gospels, the author of the *Gospel According to Thomas*, echoed that mode of thinking when he wrote, "His disciples said to him, 'Twenty-four prophets have spoken in Israel, and all of them spoke concerning you" (§52).[3] The problem has been, however, In what sense did the OT, or even parts of it, speak about Jesus, the Messiah or Christ?[4] Were such NT and later statements meant to understand OT passages as referring to Christ in their literal sense? Where would one find such OT passages? Such queries gave rise to the possibility of some other sense of the OT.

In the history of Christian theology there arose, consequently, different senses of Scripture, two of which were the most prominent: the literal sense, and the spiritual sense.[5] Others too appeared in time, such as the fuller sense and the accommodated sense. Each of the senses, however, developed problems in the understanding of them, and it is to these that I shall devote the rest of my remarks, under four headings: (1) the literal sense of Scripture; (2) the spiritual sense of Scripture; (3) the fuller sense of Scripture; and (4) the accommodated sense of Scripture.

1. The Literal Sense of Scripture

A standard, modern definition of the literal sense of Scripture runs like this: "The sense which the human author directly intended and which the written words conveyed."[6] In such a definition three elements are important: the adverb "directly," the phrase "the human author," and the clause "which the written words conveyed." "Directly" is used to prevent the meaning from being extended to the later use of the words, either in a quotation by some other author, or in a fuller sense, or in a canonical sense. "The human author" has to be understood as the last one responsible for the final form of the words in a given statement or story, whether he himself has written it (as did Luke) or dictated it (as Paul often did), or possibly used a secretary or "ghost writer" (as in 1 Peter), or in whose name a disciple may have composed something (as in the Pastoral Epistles). In antiquity, one also understood "author" as the one to whom a literary tradition was ascribed, as in the case of the Pentateuch, often called the Law of Moses. Finally, "which the written words conveyed" denotes the message that the words used carried to the first recipients of it; it thus gives priority to what has actually been written.

Such an understanding of the literal sense of Scripture is found in Pope Pius XII's encyclical *Divino afflante Spiritu*: "Let interpreters bear in mind that their foremost and greatest endeavor should be to discern and define clearly that sense of the biblical words that is called 'literal'...so that the mind of the author may be made abundantly clear."[7] The same idea is found earlier in the classic discussion of Thomas Aquinas that "the literal sense is that which the author intended."[8] Thomas also called it "sensus historicus," and subdivided it into "history, aetiology, analogy" *(historia, aetiologia, analogia)*, a distinction that creates no trouble, even though one might hesitate today to agree with some of the examples that he cited from Scripture.[9] He also recognized rightly that "the parabolic sense is contained in the literal; for something can be denoted by words properly, and something figuratively, and the literal sense is (then) not the figure, but that which is figured."[10] That means that, if Christ is called "the Lion of Judah" or "the Lamb of God" (John 1:36), he would not be an animal, a lion or a lamb, but that which "Lion of Judah" or "Lamb of God" stood for or figured. Similarly, the literal sense would include the

87

imperative "Let your loins be girt" (Luke 12:35), a metaphorical expression for the disciple's need of readiness for action. Thomas devoted a whole article to the use of metaphor in Scripture.[11] Such an understanding of the literal sense, however, has encountered a number of problems, which must be considered.

The first problem emerges when one looks at the definition of the literal sense given in the Biblical Commission's 1993 document, *The Interpretation of the Bible in the Church*, where one finds a slight difference: "The literal sense of Scripture is that which has been expressed directly by the inspired human authors."[12] The Commission was careful not to confuse the literal sense with a "literalist" sense, understood in any fundamentalistic way, and insisted on the literal meaning as that conveyed by the literary form used by the authors "according to the literary conventions of the time," and even admitted that "a story" might "not belong to the genre of history but be instead a work of imaginative fiction."[13] Such clarifications are important today, but what is striking is the absence in this definition of any reference to the intention or mind of the human author. The emphasis is rather on what "has been expressed directly."[14]

Behind this difference in the definition lies the conviction often expressed in modern literary criticism that the author's intention is immaterial or inconsequential to the meaning of a piece of literature. This has been called the "intentional fallacy" or the "fallacy of authorial intention," because it is maintained that a piece of literature can take on a meaning quite different from what the author may have intended. It can derive a meaning from the context in which it is used or from the perspective of the reader."[15] The Commission actually did not develop this aspect or even express itself on this matter, but simply restricted its definition to what "has been expressed directly," which seemed to convey sufficiently what has always been meant by the definition of the literal sense.

This difference in definition, however, calls for at least three comments. First, since we are speaking about the Bible, hence about literature that has been composed by different authors or editors over a long period of time, at least a thousand years for the span of the OT and NT, and that has been put in its final form at least nineteen hundred years ago, "the mind of the author" is not easy to ascertain. The "author" in many instances is not known, and even the time of composition in often beyond our reach.

Second, a correct analysis of what "has been expressed directly by the inspired human authors," as the Commission has phrased it, does yield in most instances something of the author's intention. One can gauge something of what the author intended from what he wrote, even if that might not correspond entirely to his intention. This is what I understand to be meant by what Thomas Aquinas and Pius XII were implying. That is the proper object of exegesis and the goal of a properly oriented historical-critical interpretation of Scripture.

Third, even though one has to reckon with the position of the New Literary Critics, who insist that a poem or other piece of literature can acquire an autonomous existence and acquire a meaning that the poet or author did not envisage, this view of literature, if applied to the Bible without some qualification, would raise a major theological problem. One might agree that some of the poetic passages of the OT — for instance, some of the Psalms — might be shown to have acquired such an independent meaning, e.g., once they were associated with others in becoming part of the Psalter. It would, however, be difficult to sustain that view for every passage in the Bible. If the meaning of a biblical text could take on a meaning different from its originally expressed — and, I would add, originally intended — meaning, then how could one say that the Bible is still the source par excellence of divine revelation, the means that God has chosen to convey to generation after generation of his people what his plans, his instructions, and his will in their regard actually are. This characteristic of the written Word of God demands that there be a basic homogeneity between what it meant and what it means, between what the inspired human author sought to express and what he did express, and what is being said by the words so read in the Church of today. This, then, is the major problem that the literal sense of Scripture raises today, and one with which theologians and exegetes have to deal.

A further problem related to the literal sense is what the Biblical Commission has called "the dynamic aspect" of the biblical message, for this message should not always be limited to "the historical circumstances" of its composition. For instance, in a royal psalm the psalmist may have been referring to the enthronement of a certain king, but what he has expressed may envisage the kingly institution as a whole, as it actually was, or as it was intended by God to be in Israel. "In this way, the text carries the reader beyond the institution of kingship in its actual historical manifestation."[16] That dynamic aspect could lead to a spiritual sense (when the Psalm might be applied to Christ [see below]), but even apart from that dimension of it this aspect is a quality of the literal sense, because it expresses the openness of the text to a broader extension of its meaning. This, then, would be an aspect of the literal sense, of which the interpreter has to be aware.

Does the biblical text have only one literal sense? The Commission answers, "In general, yes; but there is no question here of a hard and fast rule."[17] An obvious exception is poetic passages in the Bible, where the author uses words that may have a multivalent reference; or some passages of the Fourth Gospel, where a number of statements have such ambivalence. A "plurality of meaning," however, cannot be found everywhere in the Bible, and so one has to be cautious in this regard. The Commission has cited an example of double meaning from the Johannine Gospel, which calls for some comment. The Johannine passage to which it refers is 11:47–52, which reads as follows:

> [47]So the chief priests and the Pharisees convened the Sanhedrin and said, "What are we going to do? This man is performing many signs. [48]If we leave him alone, all will believe in him, and the Romans will come and take away both our land and our nation." [49]Caiaphas, who was high priest that year, said to them, "You know nothing; [50]and you do not realize that it is better for you that one man should die instead of the people, so that the whole nation may not perish." [51]He did not say this on his own, but being high priest for that year, he prophesied that Jesus was going to die for the nation, [52]and not only for the nation, but also to gather into one the dispersed children of God.

The Commission comments on this passage as follows:

> Even when a human utterance appears to have only one meaning, divine inspiration can guide the expression in such a way as to create more than one meaning. This is the

case with the saying of Caiaphas in John 11:50: at one and the same time it expresses both an immoral political ploy and a divine revelation. The two aspects belong, both of them, to the literal sense, for they are both made clear by the context.[18]

What the Commission does not make clear, however, is that the second meaning of Caiaphas's words, i.e., his prophecy, is not evident from the inspired recording of his words alone by the evangelist in v. 50. The prophetic character of Caiaphas's utterance comes rather *from the evangelist's explanation* offered in vv. 51–52: "He did not say this on his own, but being the high priest for that year, he prophesied that Jesus was going to die for the nation, and not only for the nation, but also to gather into one the dispersed children of God." Would any reader ever have come to such an understanding of Caiaphas's words in v. 50, were it not for the evangelist's added explanation? At any rate, the Commission acknowledged that this instance was "extreme," and it gave no guarantee that any other biblical texts have more than one literal meaning. It is no guarantee that all — or even other — biblical texts have more than one literal meaning. One has to insist on that, even though one may still reckon with the dynamic aspect of some texts, especially OT texts, when they are subjected to *relecture* in the NT.

The literal sense is the goal of a properly oriented historical-critical interpretation of Scripture. By "properly oriented" I mean the use of that method with the presupposition of Christian faith that one is interpreting the written Word of God couched in ancient human language, with a message not only for the people of old, but also for Christians of today.

2. The Spiritual Sense of Scripture

The problems that the spiritual sense of Scripture raises today are different and multiple, but they are almost all derived from the fact that the term "spiritual," when used of the meaning of a biblical passage, has become a weasel word. Its connotation always depends on who is using it, and one has to try to sort out its intended nuances.

First, as used by Pius XII in his encyclical of 1943, *Divino afflante Spiritu*, and by the Biblical Commission in its 1993 document, "spiritual sense" is given its traditional meaning, which is the christological sense of OT passages.[19] The spiritual sense is "the meaning expressed by the biblical texts when read, under the influence of the Holy Spirit, in the context of the paschal mystery of Christ and of the new life which flows from it....In it the New Testament recognizes the fulfillment of the Scriptures."[20] This sense of Scripture thus acknowledges a meaning of the OT at which NT writers have often hinted.[21] For instance, when Paul writes that what was said about Abraham's faith in Gen 15:6 (LXX), being accredited to him as righteousness, "Those words 'it was credited to him' were written not only for Abraham's sake, but for ours too" (Rom 4:23–24), Paul was thinking of the spiritual meaning of that OT passage. Or when Luke depicts the risen Christ saying, "All that was written about me in the Law of Moses, in the Prophets, and in the Psalms must see fulfillment" (24:44), he was interpreting the OT in a global spiritual sense. Similarly, the Epistle to the Hebrews gives a spiritual sense, when it understands Ps 2:7 of Jesus as God's Son (1:5) and Ps 8:5–7 of "Jesus 'crowned with glory and honor'...made 'for a little while lower than angels" (2:5–9).

This spiritual sense thus recognizes a unity in the written Word of God, i.e., in the OT and NT together, which the Christian interpreter has to respect. It recognizes this as a theological unity that the Church has kept alive through its living Tradition, a unity which respects the two Testaments and does not try to confuse them. It seeks rather to accord them their proper historical function and pertinence to the people of God.[22] It recognizes too that OT themes are enriched by their NT counterparts and are transformed progressively by the NT thrust.

This "spiritual sense" is called traditional because it is traced back to Origen, who certainly made it popular, if he was not the first so to label it. For he maintained that all Scripture (meaning the OT) had a spiritual *(pneumatikon)* sense, but not all of it had a bodily *(sōmatikon)* sense.[23] Origen insisted on this sense of Scripture especially in his debate with Jewish interpreters of the OT. This traditional meaning is likewise the motivation for the use of the OT in much of the Christian liturgy. In itself, this christological meaning of the OT is not problematic, even if one has to recognize that it is an added sense, i.e., added to the literal sense of the OT. Thus, it is a more-than-literal sense of the OT.

Such an understanding of the spiritual sense of the OT does not mean that the modern Christian interpreter accepts as valid all the fanciful figurative, allegorical, and typological meanings attributed to the OT by patristic writers (such as Origen and the Alexandrian School or Ambrose and Augustine). What is valid in the patristic interpretation is the continuation of the christological meaning of the OT given by inspired NT writers, since their aim was to unite the two Testaments and to draw out the deep and real meaning of the biblical text in light of the entire economy of salvation.[24] As the Biblical Commission put it, "The Fathers of the Church teach [us] to read the Bible theologically, within the heart of a living Tradition, with an authentic Christian spirit."[25] The patristic liberty in taking a phrase out of its context and producing multifarious symbolic and allegorical meanings, which the Fathers have given at times, is another matter. They are not of the essence of the spiritual sense and run "the risk of being something of an embarrassment to people of today."[26]

To this traditional understanding of the spiritual sense it seems that one would have to relegate a puzzling statement of the Commission, which wrote, "Already in the Old Testament, there are many instances where texts have a religious or spiritual sense as their literal sense. Christian faith recognizes in such cases an anticipatory relationship to the new life brought by Christ."[27] What is not clear in such a statement is, first of all, how that "anticipatory relationship" differs from the traditional christological sense of the OT. To my way of thinking, that is simply saying the same thing in another way, since the "anticipatory relationship" is really something added to the literal sense of the OT text, because of "the new life brought by Christ."

Moreover, such an understanding of the spiritual sense says nothing about what might be a "spiritual" meaning of NT passages.

The Commission also stated that, contrary to a current view, there is not necessarily a distinction between the two senses [literal and spiritual]. When a biblical text relates directly to the paschal mystery of Christ or to the new life which results from it, its literal sense is already a spiritual sense. Such is regularly the case in the NT.[28] Does that mean, then, that every verse of the NT has not only a literal but also a spiritual sense, or that the literal sense of every verse is already its spiritual sense, having a christological meaning? Why, then, distinguish them? Let us grant for the moment that that is so, there is still a further way in which the spiritual sense may have to be understood.

Does not the OT itself, apart from its added christological connotation or that "anticipatory relationship," have a spiritual sense? Another way of putting this question can be formulated in terms of the medieval four senses of Scripture. The distich of the thirteenth-century Dominican Augustine of Dacia is quoted by the Biblical Commission:

> Littera gesta docet, quid credas allegoria,
> moralis quid agas, quid speres anagogia.[29]

According to that medieval view, *littera gesta docet* (the letter teaches facts), *quid credas allegoria* (the allegorical [sense] what you are to believe), *moralis quid agas* (the moral [sense] what you are to do), *quid speres anagogia* (the anagogic [sense] what you are to hope for). Thomas Aquinas, interpreting the distich, said that the first meaning, by which words signify things, belongs to the first sense, which is the historical or literal meaning.[30] The *littera* expressed the historical meaning that the human author wanted to convey. The other three were considered subdivisions of the spiritual sense.

That medieval distich, which many quote with approval, is problematic, because it asserts that the *littera*, or "literal sense," would have nothing to do with faith or with what one is to believe. Astoundingly, it says rather that Christian faith is to be governed by the allegorical meaning of Scripture: *quid credas allegoria!*

Moreover, such an understanding of "literal sense" would seem to mean that the Hebrew Scriptures in the many centuries before the coming of Jesus of Nazareth were devoid of any spiritual meaning. And that the written Word of God in the Law, the Prophets, and the Writings had only a "historical" sense, as the medievals understood the term. Paul readily admitted that "the Jews were entrusted with the oracles of God" (Rom 3:2), but were those oracles, in their literal meaning, devoid of nourishment for the spiritual lives of the Chosen People of old?

When one reflects on this aspect of the Hebrew Scriptures, one can see how "there is not necessarily a distinction between the two senses [literal and spiritual]."[31] Indeed, in such a case the literal sense might well be the spiritual sense. For instance, in the *Shema'*, "Hear, O Israel! The LORD is our God, the LORD alone!" (Deut 6:4), the literal sense of that proposition has at once a spiritual dimension. Moreover, it is not just a spiritual sense for the Jewish people who fed their religious lives on it in the centuries before Christ, but it is still true for those Jews of today who seek to live out their ancestral faith. Moreover, it is a spiritual truth for Christians as well, for whom the OT forms part of the written Word of God. For Christians too, the literal sense of the *Shema'* is itself the spiritual sense of those words, even apart from any reference to Christ.[32]

The same would have to be said of the "spiritual" dimension of the literal meaning of the Decalogue (Exod 20:1–17; Deut 5:6–21), and of the numerous prophetic pronouncements about the care of widows and orphans, aliens and the poor (Isa 1:17; 10:2; Jer 22:3; Zech 7:10; Mal 3:5). These and other such directives in the OT are still meant to guide Christians in their religious lives, in their relation to the Lord of the Universe. The impact of such OT teaching is not governed solely by *littera gesta docet* but rather by *moralis quid agas*, by the "moral" sense, as the medievals understood the term. Again, when a Christian turns today to the Psalter and prays, "The LORD is my shepherd" (Ps 23:1), it could have a christological meaning, if "Lord" is understood in the NT sense of *Kyrios* used of the risen Christ. But the Christian could also direct that prayer to the "LORD" in the sense of the God of the OT or God the Father, and the literal sense of the metaphor used in that Psalm would be feeding the religious and spiritual life of such a Christian, as much as it would that of a devout modern Jew who would so pray.

This way in which I have just been using the term "spiritual sense" should perhaps not be so labeled. I have tried to set forth the reasons why I have used it, which may justify its use. Perhaps someone might object, however, and say that what I have described is nothing else than the "literal sense" of such OT passages and that some other term should be employed to accentuate their import, something like the "religious" import of what has been expressed literally. That may be true, but in reality it is the connotations of the medieval senses that create the problem, when *littera* is set over against *allegoria* and *moralis*. This way of using "spiritual sense" has not been given much treatment in the 1993 document of the Biblical Commission, apart from the not-too-clear statement about there not being "necessarily a distinction between the two senses."

Finally, Cardinal Dulles has admitted that

> this effort [of the Commission] to set forth the senses of Scripture will surely evoke further discussion. The distinctions are not as clear as one might hope. The three meanings [literal, spiritual, and fuller] really collapse into two since the spiritual sense is either the same as the literal, in the event that the inspired writer intended to refer to Christ and the Christian life, or else it is the same as the "fuller" sense, in the event that no such reference was intended. Among the two remaining senses, the distinction between the literal and the fuller sense is less than perspicuous. In its explanation of the literal sense the PBC calls attention to the "dynamic aspect" of many biblical texts, which are "from the start open to further developments...more or less foreseeable in advance" (80)....In view of this dynamic understanding of the literal sense, it is not easy to distinguish between the literal and the fuller sense.[33]

It is easy to agree with Dulles's appraisal in this regard, but the problem may not be solely with the 1993 document of the Biblical Commission, but with the way in which the question of the senses of Scripture has been discussed up until now. That is why I spoke of the "spiritual" sense as a weasel word. I hope at least that what I have laid out above does not obfuscate the matter still more. Dulles's discussion has raised the notion of the fuller sense of Scripture, to which I now turn.

3. The Fuller Sense of Scripture

The *sensus plenior* of Scripture is a relatively new notion. It was given serious consideration only in the first part of the twentieth century, and so it does not have the venerable status of the two senses already discussed. The term was coined by A. Fernández in 1925.[34]

The Commission has picked up this notion and defined *sensus plenior* as the "deeper meaning of the text, intended by God, but not clearly expressed by the human author."[35] It thus builds on the normal Catholic understanding of biblical inspiration according to which God is regarded as the principal author of Scripture and the inspired human writer as its secondary author. With such a distinction, it is possible that God would have moved a human writer to formulate something, the *sensus plenior* of which would have become apparent in the light of subsequent reference to or use of that formulation, and of which the human author so moved originally would have had no inkling. The Commission also expressed a cautionary qualification about the understanding of this sense: "Its existence in the biblical text comes to be known when one studies the text in the light of other biblical texts which utilize it or in its relationship with the internal development of revelation."[36] In other words, there has to be another passage in Scripture that rereads the original passage and thus reveals a further meaning of that text. For example, Matthew's words, "the virgin shall be with child" (1:23), supplies such a sense to the prophecy of Isaiah (7:14), when it uses the Greek *parthenos* (adopted from the LXX) to mean "virgin," thus giving a *sensus plenior* to ʿ*almāh*, which in the Hebrew original of Isaiah meant "young marriageable girl." Or there has to be a genuine development in the Church's dogmatic Tradition that makes known the *sensus plenior* of a biblical text. The Commission cites in this regard the patristic and conciliar teaching about the persons of the Trinity as such a sense given to the NT data about God the Father, the Son, and the Holy Spirit. Or again, the Council of Trent provided the *sensus plenior* of Paul's teaching in Rom 5:12, when it defined original sin as involved in that passage.[37] I have already mentioned the difficulty that A. Dulles finds with this example of the *sensus plenior*.[38]

The important thing about the "fuller sense" of Scripture is to realize that the Commission in no way authorizes an individual interpreter to invoke it in the explanation of any biblical text whatsoever. There is always the need of the control of further use of the text either in Scripture itself or in the dogmatic Tradition of the Church.

Lastly, the *sensus plenior* is a case where the dynamic aspect of the OT may be seen to result in a fuller meaning, as a later use of it exploits its "open" character.

4. The Accommodated Sense of Scripture

There have been times when modern writers use the term "spiritual sense" to mean an "accommodated sense" of Scripture. An "accommodated sense" is found when an interpreter uses a meaning that is not warranted by the words, phrase, or context of a passage. It is really the result of eisegesis, the opposite of exegesis — the reading of some meaning into the text.

In 1987, Pope John Paul II issued the encyclical *Redemptoris Mater* to announce the coming Marian Year of 1988.[39] In it he quoted Col 3:3, which exhorts the Christians of Colossae to think of what is above, "for you have died, and your life is hidden with Christ in God," expressing the share in the glorious life of Christ that is their destiny as righteous Christians. John Paul II, however, used the verse rather of Mary living with Jesus during the so-called Hidden Life: "During the years of Jesus' hidden life in the house at Nazareth, Mary's life, too, is 'hid with Christ in God' (Col. 3:3) through faith." That use of Col 3:3 may be suitable for a papal "biblical meditation," as Cardinal Joseph Ratzinger called the encyclical,[40] but it is nothing more than an "accommodation" of the biblical text, foisting on it a meaning that neither the principal nor the secondary author of that verse of Colossians ever intended or expressed. This and other accommodated meanings of biblical texts should not be called the "spiritual sense," as some have done. In such a case, it would be another example of how "spiritual" sense has become a weasel word.

Conclusion

I terminate this discussion of the senses of Scripture by quoting a few lines once written by the theologian Cardinal Dulles:

> My own present leaning would be toward a method [of biblical interpretation] that makes use of historical-critical studies to assure a solid foundation in the biblical sources themselves, but does so under the continuous guidance of tradition and magisterial teaching. An adequate theological use of Scripture, I believe, would build also on the achieve-

ments of biblical theology and the kind of spiritual exegesis described above [referring to his description of biblical interpretation set forth by L. Bouyer, H. de Lubac, H. U. von Balthasar]. An interpretation that limited itself to the historical-critical phase would overlook the tacit meanings conveyed by the biblical stories, symbols, and metaphors. A comprehensive approach, combining scientific and spiritual exegesis, does better justice to Catholic tradition and the directives of Vatican II, and better serves the needs of systematic theology.[41]

I have no difficulty with what Dulles says about the use of the historical-critical method along with the continuous guidance of tradition and the magisterium; that would be included in what I mean by the properly oriented use of the method. Nor do I find anything problematic in his implied references to literary, rhetorical, and narrative refinements of that method. Properly oriented historical-critical interpretation of the Bible would include what he calls biblical theology and the tacit meanings of biblical stories, symbols, and metaphors. I would hesitate, however, to include what he calls "spiritual exegesis," for some of the reasons already set forth above in this discussion, but especially because I find that a misuse of terminology. What Dulles is calling for, along with theologians such as L. Bouyer, H. de Lubac, H. U. von Balthasar, and others, is a realization that the written Word of God is not only addressed to the people of old, to the people of the First Covenant or to the new people of God in early Christian centuries, but that it also is addressed to Christians of today. It is, in effect, God's Word to us here and now. What Dulles means by "spiritual exegesis" is nothing more than the actualized literal sense of Scripture as ascertained by the properly oriented historical-critical method, as I have tried to set forth in chapter 4. God speaks to his people today through the inspired written Word, when its literal sense so ascertained is duly actualized.

These, then, are various problems about the meaning of Scripture involved in the interpretation of the Bible today. They make known to us the many ways in which one has to cope with the "truth" of the Bible. That biblical truth is not univocal, but rather analogous. As truth for Christians, it has to be normed by the literal and spiritual senses of the inspired written Word, and at times even by its fuller sense. For these senses make known to us what the written Word of God means and reveals, and how that Word stands for us as *norma normans non normata*, "the norm that norms" our Christian lives, which is itself "not normed." Along with the written Word of Scripture, the dogmatic Tradition of the Church also plays a role in that normative and revelatory process, but it is *norma normata*, "the norm that is normed," i.e., by Scripture, out of which it has grown.[42]

7

RAYMOND E. BROWN, S.S., RENOWNED REPRESENTATIVE OF BIBLICAL SCHOLARSHIP

Finally, this discussion of the modes of interpreting Scripture finds a fitting conclusion in the way that Raymond E. Brown, S.S., interpreted Scripture, not only in the good that he achieved by it, but also in the way he was maligned for it. There is good reason to recall the significance of his interpretative work.

I can no longer recall when I first met Raymond Brown, but it must have been in the autumn of 1953. I had just returned from Europe, where I had studied at Louvain in Belgium and at Münster in Germany, and was beginning my doctoral studies at the Johns Hopkins University in Baltimore. At that time, Brown had just been ordained and was spending the first year of his priestly life teaching at St. Charles College, the minor seminary run by the Sulpicians in Catonsville, Maryland. The following year he joined us at Hopkins, as he began his own studies for the Ph.D. So we were fellow students at Hopkins, and thus began a lifelong friendship, which ended only with his untimely death on 8 August 1998.

Those forty-five years, filled with great friendship, were years when we lived for a while nearby, he at St. Mary's Seminary in Baltimore, and I at Woodstock College in Woodstock, Maryland, about ten miles away. There were also years when we were separated by considerable distances, but we kept in touch constantly by letter and telephone. We learned to collaborate on various projects, the translation-committee of the New American Bible, the editorship of *The Jerome Biblical Commentary* of 1968 and of *The New Jerome Biblical Commentary* of 1990. We worked together, along with others, in the production of other books, *Peter in the New Testament* of 1973 and *Mary in the New*

Testament of 1978. All that collaboration has now come to an end by his unexpected death.

My further remarks about Raymond Brown and his significance will be made under three headings: (1) Brown's contribution to biblical scholarship; (2) Brown's role in ecumenical work and church life; and (3) the unjust criticism and persecution of Brown.

1. Brown's Contribution to Biblical Scholarship

The name of Raymond Brown will long be recalled for the mark that he made on biblical scholarship, not only in this country but in the world at large. It was not for nothing that the magazine *Time* once hailed him as "probably the premier Catholic Scripture scholar in the U.S." For he arrived on the scene as a young scholar just as the revolutionary encyclical of Pope Pius XII was beginning to seep into American Catholic life and just as the remarkable discovery of the Dead Sea Scrolls was beginning to break upon the world. He made his mark in biblical scholarship by making the most of these two important events that affected the study of the Bible in the twentieth century.

In 1943, in the midst of the Second World War, when the minds of most people were preoccupied with other things than the interpretation of the Bible, Pope Pius XII had issued his encyclical *Divino afflante Spiritu* on the promotion of biblical studies. For that reason the revolution, which that encyclical was to cause in Catholic Church, was delayed for almost a decade, and even longer in the United States.[1] That encyclical made a major break from the often allegorical or fundamentalistic interpretation of Scripture that had been in vogue in Catholic interpretation from at least medieval times. Although Pius XII never used the term "historical-critical method" in his encyclical, that term accurately describes what he was advocating and what Brown adopted for his interpretation of Scripture.

When Brown began his university study of Scripture in 1954, he joined us in the study of Semitic languages, ancient history, and Near Eastern archaeology at Hopkins, under the tutelage of the famous Palestinian archaeologist and biblical scholar William Foxwell Albright. The name of Albright had become so famous that it attracted not only Brown, but many others, who eventually became noted

Scripture scholars or biblical archaeologists: G. Ernest Wright, Frank M. Cross, David N. Freedman, Thomas O. Lambdin, William L. Moran, Mitchell J. Dahood, many of whom came to teach at either Harvard University or the Biblical Institute in Rome.

Brown was a staunch advocate of the historical-critical method of interpreting Scripture. He not only used it in his commentaries on the Johannine Gospel and Epistles, but also advocated and defended the use of that method in such books as *The Critical Meaning of the Bible*[2] and *Biblical Exegesis and Church Doctrine*.[3]

Once Brown began to teach at St. Mary's Seminary in Baltimore in 1959, a year after I began to teach at Woodstock College, he started in earnest his publishing career. Many books, articles, and reviews subsequently flowed from his pen, and the bibliography of his writings has been compiled.[4] It is easy to recall the main works with which he made a noteworthy impact on the scholarly world of biblical studies. They were his two-volume commentary, *The Gospel according to John* (1966 and 1970),[5] which not only built on earlier Johannine scholarship, but introduced many new insights and made use of the new literature of the Dead Sea Scrolls to illuminate that Gospel. Later came his commentary on *The Epistles of John* (1982),[6] in which he developed his idea of the Johannine school, an idea that he and J. Louis Martyn, his colleague at Union Theological Seminary, had often discussed together. In *The Birth of the Messiah* (1977),[7] Brown presented an extended and detailed study of the infancy narratives of the Gospels according to Matthew and Luke. Later two volumes were published by him on *The Death of the Messiah* (1994),[8] in which he presented a detailed analysis of the passion narratives of the four Gospels. His last great work, *An Introduction to the New Testament* (1997),[9] was a comprehensive approach to all the books of the NT. That book became the fitting crown not only of his publications, but also of his long career as a biblical scholar, for he was widely acclaimed for his perceptive analysis, clarity of expression, and intellectual integrity. In all these major books, Brown sought to maintain a centrist position, as he himself liked to call his approach, never proposing wild ideas or idiosyncratic opinions, as did some of his American colleagues. Brown's interpretations of Scripture were always carried out in the service of the Church, and that has not gone unnoticed, for a recent writer has studied what he calls "the ecclesial hermeneutic of Raymond E. Brown."[10]

There were, moreover, less bulky publications that made their mark as well on the scholarly world.[11] Brown also sought constantly to bring his scholarly expertise to the level of the general reader in the publication of many paperbacks and popular books. Such, for example, was his booklet *An Adult Christ at Christmas*, which sought to explain the Matthean and Lucan infancy narratives for adult readers in a clear and intelligent way. Other paperbacks centered on feasts or periods of the Church's liturgical calendar, Advent, Lent, or Easter; they sought to bring a biblical understanding to such feasts.

Although Brown began his biblical teaching career at the Sulpician seminary of St. Mary's in Baltimore from 1959 to 1970, he ended it as the Auburn Distinguished Professor of Biblical Studies, when he retired from Union Theological Seminary in New York in 1990. There he had taught from 1971 to 1990. Thus, true to his vocation as a Sulpician, he trained many seminarians who became diocesan priests. He also educated Jesuit scholastics for a few years at Woodstock College, when it moved to New York City and was affiliated with Union Theological Seminary. But, above all, he likewise educated many, many non-Catholic students at that Seminary itself during his twenty-year tenure there. So both Catholic and non-Catholic students of theology were fortunate to have as a Scripture professor a man who was an excellent teacher, noted for his clarity, integrity of judgment, and fairness to all issues and persons. Though he was a man, he advocated in a balanced way many matters of special concern to women in those years of his teaching at Union Theological Seminary, and many female students have lauded his encouragement of them to pursue graduate biblical studies so that they too could play a role in what had previously been a male-dominated world of scholarship.

During his years of teaching at St. Mary's in Baltimore, Brown realized the need of a one-volume commentary on the Bible that followed the directives of Pius XII's encyclical and used the historical-critical method of interpreting Scripture. In his teaching there, he had to use at first *A Catholic Commentary on Holy Scripture*,[12] which was mainly the product of retrograde British Catholic biblical scholarship and horribly out of date even from the day of its first publication. In order to put a more adequate textbook in the hands of seminarian-students, Brown and Roland E. Murphy conceived the idea of a new one-volume commentary on Scripture. About the same time, I, at Woodstock College, was trying to launch a badly needed multivolume Catholic commentary on the NT, but I had little success in rounding up potential authors. So I eagerly joined Brown and Murphy in their project, when invited. They were already in contact with Prentice-Hall, the eventual publisher of *The Jerome Biblical Commentary*. After a number of stormy years spent in prodding procrastinating contributors, we managed to publish the *JBC* in December of 1968.[13] Despite its size and technical character, it soon became a best-seller, not only in the textbook world, but also on the popular market. Eventually, it was reprinted in a cheaper edition for Catholics of India and Ceylon (Sri Lanka), pirated in Taiwan, and translated into Spanish and Italian.[14] In English alone, it sold over 300,000 copies in this country and Canada. Brown was the editor of the general articles, and thus his example and influence contributed in many ways to the excellence of that part of the *JBC*. So in this indirect way, Brown contributed to the biblical education of many, many persons in the world at large. These were not only Catholics, but also many Protestants, because the *JBC* came to be used in a number of Protestant seminaries across the English-speaking world. Although Brown was reluctant to undertake a revision of the *JBC*, he eventually yielded to the pressure of Murphy and myself, and so he contributed his invaluable services again to *The New Jerome Biblical Commentary* of 1990.[15]

Brown also began his biblical studies just as the discovery of the Dead Sea Scrolls was breaking upon the world. In this area too, he made his contribution in a small way. After he had finished his doctoral studies at Johns Hopkins in 1958, he was named a Fellow at the American School of Oriental Research in Jerusalem, as it was then called, with a special designation to work on the concordance of non-biblical texts from Qumran Cave 4 that was being put together. I had been the first Fellow so appointed in 1957–1958 and started the concordance; Brown followed me in 1958–1959, and W. G. Oxtoby followed him in 1959–1960. In those days, we had no computers, and all the cards were written by hand. Such a concordance was badly needed by the seven-member editorial team appointed to piece together, study, and publish the thousands of fragments from Qumran Cave 4. It was meant to help them in identifying tiny fragments, relating them to others, and translating them. There was also the plan that, once the fragmentary texts of Cave 4 were all published, we would be able to revise the tentative readings on the cards according to their final and definitive form and publish the concordance. Alas, in 2007 we are still awaiting the final publication of some of the fragmentary texts, and the concordance is now being produced with a computer systematically, as each volume in the series Discoveries in the Judaean Desert is published by the Clarendon Press of Oxford. The cards of our concordance, however, were eventually photographed in the late 1980s, printed in a restricted edition, and sent to those few editors to whom the fragments of Cave 4 had been originally entrusted for publication. Neither Brown nor I ever received a copy of that concordance, despite all the work that we had put into it! That concordance, however, not only helped those few original editors, but was assisting many others who more recently have been co-opted into the editorial team to speed up the publication of those important texts of Qumran Cave 4. Brown never published much on the Dead Sea Scrolls, but he did contribute an important survey article on them in both the *JBC* and the *NJBC*.

So much for Brown's remarkable contributions to the world of biblical scholarship.

2. Brown's Role in Ecumenical Work and Church Life

Almost as important as his biblical work was Brown's activity in Church life and in ecumenical endeavors, because in these areas he served the Church on a far wider level than in his biblical contributions.

To the dismay of many ultraconservative Catholics in the United States, Pope Paul VI appointed Raymond Brown as the American member to the newly reconstituted Pontifical Biblical Commission for the term 1972–1978.[16] Paul VI had restructured the Commission in 1971, getting rid of the cardinals, who had previously been the only members of the Commission,[17] and bringing in as members twenty biblical scholars from across the world to advise him and the Vatican congregations in matters pertaining to the Bible. They were said to be persons "outstanding for their learning, prudence, and Catholic regard for the Magisterium of the Church." Thus Brown became one of the *electi quidem* in the Catholic world of biblical matters, the only American of that first group of twenty members of the Biblical Commission. Subsequently, after I had finished two terms on that Commission in 1995, he was named as my successor in 1996 and was completing his second term when he died. He served in this capacity, having been recommended for it by the episcopal conference of the United States. Such was the confidence of the American bishops in him that they proposed his name for a second time, despite all the criticism of Brown's interpretation of Scripture by conservative Catholics.[18]

In the years following the Second Vatican Council, when the Catholic bishops of the United States appointed a team to engage in theological dialogue with American Lutherans, Brown was one of that first team. The Catholic and Lutheran theologians met for the first time in Baltimore in July 1965. Because it was the first time in almost four hundred and twenty-five years that Catholic and Lutheran theologians were sitting down together to discuss their differences, a neutral topic was chosen: The Nicene Creed as Dogma of the Church.[19] It was expected that there would be a wide consensus between the two teams on such a topic, and that proved to be true, as they also mapped out areas of further necessary discussion and study on divisive issues.

The second round of the dialogue took place in 1966 and was devoted to Baptism. For it Brown contributed a paper, "One Baptism for the Remission of Sins," with a Lutheran paper on an aspect of the same subject by Krister Stendahl, the Swedish-born dean of the Harvard Divinity School.[20] There was again hardly any disagreement between the two teams of theologians on this topic.

The third round was devoted to Eucharist as Sacrifice,[21] and it was thought that the two sides would be beginning a dialogue on a neuralgic and divisive topic. However, to the surprise of all, there was a remarkable agreement between the two sides, despite the controversy between Lutherans and Catholics since the days of the Reformation and the Council of Trent about the sacrificial nature of the Mass and about the nature of the Eucharist or Lord's Supper. Once the tenets of each side were explained properly about Sacrifice and Real Presence, little area for disagreement was found, despite a difference of terminology. Since this topic was more theological and historical than biblical, there was little that was asked of Brown, but he made his contribution to the general theological discussion.

The fourth topic, Eucharist and Ministry, was the beginning of the really controversial matters that still separate Lutherans and Catholics.[22] On this topic, Brown again made his contribution to the general discussion, and the biblical paper on the Catholic side was prepared by Jerome D. Quinn of the Seminary of St. Paul in St. Paul, Minnesota. The common statement on Eucharist and ministry proved to be the most controversial of all the papers that were issued by the National Dialogue. Though it clarified many divisive points, the topic to which it was devoted remains today a much-debated and sensitive issue between Lutherans and Catholics, not only in this country but in the world at large.

Papal Primacy and Universal Church was the topic of the fifth round of the national dialogue.[23] For this topic the question of Peter's role in the NT was obviously very important. Because the discussion of the Petrine function was foreseen to be technical and too much to be discussed by the theologians in the plenary sessions of the dialogue, a decision was made to have Brown gather a task force of Catholic and non-Catholic scholars to prepare a study on Peter in the NT. This was officially sponsored by the National Dialogue and resulted in the small book *Peter in the New Testament*, an assessment of the NT data by Catholic and Protestant scholars.[24] The participants in the task force were not only Catholics and Lutherans, but also other non-Lutheran Protestant NT scholars, because Brown insisted on the value of voices from the non-Lutheran Protestant traditions on this topic: he realized that the Petrine role in the NT would affect many other bilateral conversations that the Catholic Church in this country would engage in. This book, when finally published, proved to be very important. It not only fed into the common statement on papal primacy, but it was translated into Dutch, French, German, Italian, Japanese, and Spanish.[25] Thus Brown's influence reached many Catholics and Protestants throughout the world.

When the common statement on papal primacy was finally finished, Brown asked to be excused from further participation in the National Dialogue with the Lutherans, and 1973 thus proved to be the last year that he was so involved. However, because he knew that the question of Mary would eventually be taken up in the Dialogue of Lutherans and Catholics, he proposed that the Dialogue sponsor a similar task force to discuss the NT data on the Blessed Virgin Mary, even in advance of the round of the Dialogue that would take up that topic. The work of that task force resulted in another small book, *Mary in the NewTestament*,[26] which was likewise translated into several modern languages.[27] Thus Brown's influence in the National Dialogue continued for a while after he was no longer a member of it. I was appointed to take his place on that Dialogue in 1973.[28]

Brown had asked to be excused from the National Lutheran-Catholic Dialogue, because by 1973 he was already involved in other time-consuming ecumenical endeavors with the World Council of Churches. As early as 1963 he had been the first Roman Catholic to be invited to address the Fourth World Conference on *Faith and Order*, which met in Montreal. He made a point of mentioning not only the advances in Catholic ecumenical relations since the time of Pope John XXIII, but also the impact that "modern critical biblical studies" in the Catholic Church were finally making in ecumenical circles. And rightly so, because it was not only the impact that the Second Vatican Council was making on the Protestants of the world, but also the revolutionary direction that Pope Pius XII had given to Catholic biblical studies in his encyclical *Divino afflante Spiritu* of 1943. For that encyclical not only came to be the springboard that prepared the Catholic Church for the Council, but it also made Protestants aware of the way that Catholics were now interpreting their favorite book, the Bible — in a way quite similar to their own.

At that Fourth World Conference on *Faith and Order*, which took place in the middle of the Council, Brown read a paper entitled "The Unity and Diversity in New Testament Ecclesiology,"[29] and debated the topic with the noted German NT scholar Ernst Käsemann, who was invited also to address the same conference. Brown's involvement with the World Conference on *Faith and Order* continued for at least twenty-five years; he was the only American Catholic member of the Faith and Order Commission by an agreement between the Vatican Secretariat and the World Council of Churches and played a major role in the statement on *Baptism, Eucharist and Ministry* issued by that Commission in 1982.[30] His early death has thus deprived the Christian ecumenical and interfaith movements of this century of one of its best and most sympathetic advocates.

By papal nomination, Brown also served as a consultor to the Vatican Secretariat for Promoting Christian Unity from 1968 to 1973, and in 1982 he was appointed by the same Secretariat to the International Methodist/Roman Catholic Dialogue.

Brown's role in Church life also included his ministry of the Word, for he was always an effective preacher. His homilies and sermons were usually expository, as he sought to explain the sometimes difficult passages of Scripture. He was invariably a corrective preacher, who made it clear in such homilies that he did not agree with certain interpretations that were at times being propounded. He sought only to elucidate the literal meaning of the written Word of God and to bring it to the level of those who listened to him. In this regard, I recall the words of Cardinal Mahony, the archbishop of Los Angeles, who told about an experience during a pilgrimage to the Holy Land in 1978, when Brown was the annual professor at the Albright Archaeological Institute in Jerusalem and when he accompanied the pilgrims to the traditional site of Jesus' Sermon on the Mount: "Father Brown gave such an elegant and reflective description of that event that, once he had finished, no one spoke or moved. We all sat there as if we had heard Jesus speaking those words for the first time."[31]

3. The Unjust Criticism and Persecution of Raymond Brown

Timothy Cardinal Manning, an earlier archbishop of Los Angeles, once said of Raymond Brown, "He is a good and holy priest, and loyal to the Church. He is a Scripture scholar and limits his skill to his Scripture expertise. Fr. Brown, as a follower of Christ, is in good company when it comes to being criticized."[32] The cardinal wrote that, as he counseled the people and priests of the Los Angeles archdiocese, "Do not be led astray by the venomous critics of Fr. Brown." Those remarks were made after Brown had become the object of severe criticism and protests, when he was invited to give the keynote address to the National Catholic Educational Association, which held its annual convention in April 1973 in New Orleans. Such a reaction to him occurred at other places too (e.g., in Anaheim, California, which eventually occasioned the remarks of Cardinal Manning).

Since the death of Brown, many have recalled the great things that he had achieved in his lifetime, and many have been the deserved eulogies of this renowned Scripture scholar. Because the "venomous" criticism of him had died down somewhat in the last decade before he died, it is all too easy to forget what an ordeal he went through in the 1970s and 1980s. The criticism of those who attacked him stemmed from a pettiness that could not brook either the notoriety that Brown had begun to enjoy or the good effect of his teaching and writing about the written Word of God on American Catholics, and indeed on Catholics and Protestants of the whole world.

Lest one forget Brown's ordeal and fail to understand the source of it, I should like to recall a few details of that sniping and unfair criticism of him. The sad thing about it is that so much of it came from fellow priests, who should have known better.

The most extended criticism and persecution came from a priest-sociologist, Msgr. George A. Kelly, a professor at St. John's University in New York. In his book, *The New Biblical Theorists: Raymond E. Brown and Beyond*,[33] Msgr. Kelly alleged that Brown had "changed both his style and his opinions in fifteen years" (p. 116), had unduly limited "the data he w[ould] accept as persuasive" (p. 121), and had "not been thoroughly evaluated by his peers" (p. 123); but also that he wrote "as if Scriptura Sola" were the "prevailing norm for Catholic exegesis" (p. 127), that Brown's "rhetoric in public controversy frequently obscure[d] the issues in scholarly dispute" (p. 129), and that he was "overprotected by American bishops" (p. 137). These were the six points that Kelly sought to make in his book about Brown.

Although that attack of Kelly was the most extended, it was not the most vicious. Some examples of the latter may help to make my point. In 1973 the periodical *Triumph* printed the following paragraph among its editorials:

Personal
Situation wanted: Are you a prestigious university, looking for an internationally known Scripture scholar with no dogmatic hang-ups? Then I'm the man for you. You'll never catch me affirming the virginal conception of Christ, the existence of Adam and Eve, the inerrancy of Jesus's knowledge, the Apostolic Succession. Do I make faith subservient to theology? deny the validity of past formulations of doctrine? deny literal truth to the Gospels? Yes, yes and

yes again. We could make beautiful heresy together. Salary? Sufficient to support me in the style to which I have become accustomed. Reply to R. E. Brown, *New York Review*, Box 47.

Mr. R. E. Brown, *New York Review*, Box 47. Dear Mr. Brown: We love you. Come home. (signed) The Catholic University of America.[34]

Catholic University had, of course, nothing to do with that editorial!

A few months later a more extended editorial, which complained about an action taken by the Catholic Biblical Association against publications such as *Triumph* included the following paragraph:

His [Manuel Miguens's] was a scholarly case,[35] so airtight that it was never dealt with by Father Brown or his claque [other similarly-thinking Catholic biblical scholars], who wouldn't renounce their faith in Brown if an archaeological find were to be dug up tomorrow saying "Raymond Brown, who will go about during the twentieth century, is a fraud," signed/Jesus of Nazareth, and attested to by a notary public.[36]

To such unfair criticism one would have to add the continuous attacks on Brown in *The Wanderer*, written by such persons as the Rev. Robert E. Burns, C.S.P.,[37] the Rev. Juniper B. Carol, O.F.M.,[38] Stanley Interrante,[39] William H. Marshner,[40] A. J. Matt, Jr.,[41] Frank Morriss,[42] John J. Mulloy,[43] Charles R. Pulver,[44] et al. Equally intemperate were the attacks on Brown that appeared in the *National Catholic Register*, written by Paul H. Hallett,[45] and the Rev. William G. Most.[46]

Brown suffered much from such unjust and vicious persecution during his scholarly life. I say this because he often complained to me personally about the way he was being vilified, and yet he never answered in kind. He never descended to the low level of his critics. It is thus an aspect of his life that one should never forget.

As I consider this persecution in Brown's life, I cannot help but think of another great Scripture scholar who likewise suffered much from his contemporaries, who never saw as clearly as he did the advantages to the Catholic Church and its teachings that could come from the historical-critical method of interpreting Scripture. I am referring to Marie-Joseph Lagrange, O.P. (1855–1938), the founder of the famous École Biblique in Jerusalem and of the highly esteemed biblical periodical, the *Revue Biblique*.[47] Now that the cause for the beatification of Lagrange has been started and his life's work is being reviewed, we realize not only how much Lagrange suffered, but also how much good he had done. His small book *La méthode historique*[48] showed how the historical-critical method could be properly used by Catholic interpreters of Scripture. It caused in his day, however, much concern among reactionary elements in the Catholic Church and even from the Consistorial Congregation of the Vatican itself.[49] The opposition to Lagrange was led above all, sad to say, by a Belgian Jesuit, A.-J. Delattre,[50] and Lagrange was eventually forbidden by Vatican authorities to teach and publish further on the OT. So he turned to the study of the NT, and his commentaries on the four Gospels remain today weighty tomes that are still consulted with profit, even though they may be a bit out of date. In Lagrange's case, the persecution was more severe than it was in Brown's; but in both it was unjust and stemmed basically from what can only be described as willful ignorance. Times have changed, and what was once considered modernist and bordering on heresy in biblical matters in Lagrange's day has become the perfectly accepted mode of interpreting Scripture in the Catholic Church today. Even the Biblical Commission of that Church insisted in 1993 that "the historical-critical method is the indispensable method for the scientific study of the meaning of ancient texts" and that Scripture as "the 'Word of God in human language'…not only admits the use of this method but actually requires it."[51]

Because of such persecution of biblical interpreters like Lagrange, Pius XII included in his encyclical of 1943 the noteworthy counsel quoted above (p. 33). Alas, those words of Pius XII were not heeded in the case of Raymond Brown. Even the notice of his death in *The Wanderer* bore the headline, "Fr. Raymond Brown, Modernist Scripture Scholar, Dead at 70."[52] The following week, *The Wanderer* carried its final attack on him, "Traditional Scholars Long Opposed Fr. Brown's Theories."[53] The "traditional scholars" in that title were the editors and writers of that notorious *Käseblättchen*. One wonders whether they ever heard of the Christian principle, *Nil nisi bonum de mortuis*!

Conclusion

By way of conclusion, it is good to recall some other highlights in Brown's life. He pursued his preparatory studies for the priesthood in Washington, DC, at the Catholic University of America, in Rome at the Gregorian University, and in Baltimore at St. Mary's Seminary. He held an M.A. in philosophy from Catholic University, an S.T.D. from St. Mary's Seminary, a Ph.D. from the Johns Hopkins University, and an S.S.L. from the Pontifical Biblical Commission.

He was honored with more than thirty honorary doctorates: from such foreign institutions as the Universities of Edinburgh (1972), Uppsala (1974), Louvain (1976), and Glasgow (1978); and from such American institutions as De Paul University (1974), Villanova University (1975), Boston College (1977), Fordham University (1977), Hofstra University (1985), and the Catholic University of America (1989). He had been a visiting professor at the Biblical Institute in Rome (1973). His book *The Virginal Conception and Bodily Resurrection of Jesus*, which seemed so controversial to some Catholics, was recommended by the American Catholic bishops among suggested readings in the bibliography of their national pastoral letter on Mary (November 1973).

In 1983 he was elected to the American Academy of Arts and Sciences. He was also the first American Catholic to have served as president of all three of the distinguished biblical societies: the Catholic Biblical Association of America (1971–72), the Society of Biblical Literature, which is the largest association of biblical scholars in the world (1976–77), and Studiorum Novi Testamenti Societas, the prestigious international NT society (1986–87). These posts constituted a recognition not only of his work as a biblical scholar, but also of his person as a churchman of no little stature.

Finally, to those of us who knew Raymond Brown as a friend, his example will always be recalled: his fidelity to the Church that he served, his gentle tolerance of those who disagreed with him, and his utmost forbearance of those who persecuted him. Brown's absolute dedication to the study of the written Word of God will never be forgotten.

8
CONCLUDING REMARKS

What I have written in the preceding seven essays amounts to a description of the methods of interpreting Scripture, its problems and controversies, and an attempt to show the need to recognize the use of a properly oriented historical-critical method of interpreting the Bible. In other words, I have been dealing with the past and the present of such interpretation, especially as it has developed in the United States of America. It is only a small part of a much larger picture that has been sketched already in the important book of G. P. Fogarty, *American Catholic Biblical Scholarship: A History from the Early Republic to Vatican II.*[1] I have composed these essays in the hope that what has happened in the past in the area of biblical interpretation may be a deterrent from repeating some of the same errors and mistakes that marked the end of the nineteenth century and most of the twentieth. I have said little about the future of biblical interpretation, except to maintain that it can never dispense with the historical-critical method.

This also means that I have said practically nothing about the future of Catholic biblical scholarship. The reason for this omission is that I am leaving that issue to others. We have seen recently the beginning of such prognostication in the book of L. T. Johnson and W. S. Kurz, *The Future of Catholic Biblical Scholarship: A Constructive Conversation.*[2] Their book has evoked already further discussion of the topic, e.g., by F. J. Matera, "The Future of Catholic Biblical Scholarship: Balance and Proportion."[3] It is certainly not the end of such conversation. Nor is it the end of the controversy that biblical interpretation, and especially the historical-critical mode of practicing it, has encountered. I shall be happy if the topics treated in these seven essays of mine help that conversation to proceed as it should.

NOTES

Chapter One: The Second Vatican Council and the Role of the Bible in Catholic Life

1. DH 2502.
2. DH 2480.
3. DH 2481.
4. ASS 26 (1893–94) 279–92 (DH 3280–94; Béchard, SD, 37–61).
5. On these discoveries, see further below, pp. 79–80.
6. ASS 35 (1902–3) 234–38 (Béchard, SD, 62–66).
7. See further J. R. Donahue, "A Journey Remembered: Catholic Biblical Scholarship 50 Years after *Divino afflante Spiritu*," *America* 169 (1993) 6–11; G. J. Hamilton, "*Divino afflante Spiritu*: Catholic Interpretation of Scripture," *Canadian Catholic Review* [Saskatoon] 6 (1988) 171–76; R. Martin-Achard, "Le renouveau biblique dans le catholicisme romain," *Revue de théologie et de philosophie* 10 (1960) 285–97; K. D. Stephenson, "Roman Catholic Biblical Scholarship: Its Ecclesiastical Context in the Past Hundred Years," *Encounter* 33 (1972) 303–28.
8. AAS 58 (1966) 817–36 (DH 4201–35; Béchard, SD, 19–33).
9. See further A. Dulles, "The Constitution on Divine Revelation in Ecumenical Perspective," *AER* 154 (1966) 217–31, esp. 220.
10. Béchard, SD, 24.
11. Béchard, SD, 128–30.
12. Béchard, SD, 23.
13. Béchard, SD, 27–28.
14. *Sancta Mater Ecclesia: Instructio de historica Evangeliorum veritate*, AAS 56 (1964) 712–18, dated 21 April 1964 (DH 4402–7; EB §§644–59; Béchard, SD 227–34).
15. Béchard, SD, 29.
16. AAS 58 (1966) 723—It has also been used in the International Theological Commission's document "De interpretatione dogmatum," *Gregorianum* 72 (1991) 5–37, esp. 24 (c.1.1).

17. *ASS* 26 (1893–94) 283; cf. Benedict XV, *Spiritus Paraclitus, AAS* 12 (1920) 409 (*EB* §483; Béchard, *SD* 100 [§13]).

18. Pope Leo XIII, however, was not the first to use the idea of Scripture as the soul of theology, since it has recently been traced back to the seventeenth century, when it was used in Decree 15 of the Thirteenth General Congregation of the Society of Jesus, held at Rome in 1687: *ut anima ipsa verae theologiae.* See *Decreta Canones Censurae et Praecepta Congregationum Generalium Societatis Iesu* (3 vols.; Avignon: F. Seguin, 1830), 1:262; J. W. Padberg et al., *For Matters of Greater Moment: The First Thirty Jesuit General Congregations: A Brief History and a Translation of Decrees* (St. Louis, MO: Institute of Jesuit Sources, 1994) 357. Cf. J. M. Lera, "Sacrae paginae studium sit veluti anima Sacrae Theologiae (Notas sobre el origen y procedencia de esta frase)," in *Palabra y vida: Homenaje a J. Alonso Díaz...* (ed. A. Vargas Machuca and G. Ruiz: Madrid: UPCM, 1984) 409–22. Also R. LaFontaine (ed.), *L'Écriture âme de la théologie* (Collection IET 9; Brussels: Institut d'Études Théologiques, 1990).

19. *Stimmen der Zeit* 168 (1961) 241–62; repr. in *Schriften der Theologie* (16 vols.; Einsiedeln: Benziger, 1954–84) 5 (1964) 82–111; in English, "Exegesis and Dogmatic theology," *Theological Investigations* (21 vols.; Baltimore, MD: Helicon; New York: Crossroad, 1961–88) 5 (1966) 67–83, esp. 70–74.

20. Ibid., 77.

21. See K. Rahner, "Scripture and Theology," *Theological Investigations* 6 (Baltimore, MD: Helicon, 1969) 89–97, esp. 93; cf. his article, "Bible, B. Theology," *Sacramentum Mundi* (6 vols.; New York: Herder & Herder, 1968–70), 1:171–78, esp. 176–77.

22. Rahner, "Scripture and Theology," 92.

23. *L'Interprétation de la Bible dans l'Eglise*, 21 September 1993 (Vatican City: Libreria Editrice Vaticana, 1993); also in *Bib* 74 (1993) 451–528. It was published simultaneously by the same publisher in English, French, German, Italian, Portuguese, and Spanish. The English translation appeared also in *Origins* 23:29 (6 January 1994) 497–524 (available from the United States Catholic Conference [Washington, DC] and, in pamphlet form, from St. Paul Books & Media [Boston, MA]); see also Béchard, *SD*, 244–317. I published a book about it, *The Biblical Commission's Document "The Interpretation of the Bible in the Church": Text and Commentary* (Subsidia biblica 18; Rome: Biblical Institute Press, 1995; available in the USA through Chicago, IL: Loyola University Press). For details about the contents of this document, see pp. 77–84.

24. See further R. E. Murphy, "Reflections on 'Actualization' of the Bible," *BTB* 26 (1996) 79–81.

25. See K. Scholtissek, "Relecture — Zu einem neu entdeckten Programmwort der Schriftauslegung (mit Blick auf das Johannesevangelium)," *Bibel und Liturgie* 70 (1997) 309–15.

26. Augustine, *Sermons* 179.1; *PL* 38:966.

27. Jerome, *Comm. in Isaiam* 1.1 Prologue; *PL* 24:17.

Chapter Two: A Roman Scripture Controversy

1. Augustine, *Ep.* 71.5 (*CSEL* 34:253; translated in *Fathers of the Church* 12:327). Even Augustine suspected the motives of the Jews who gave the African bishop that information: "Was it out of ignorance or malice that they replied that what the Greek and Latin manuscripts read and said was (also) found in the Hebrew?" (ibid.; my translation).

2. Augustine, *Ep.* 71.5; *CSEL* 34:253.

3. The Hebrew word in the Masoretic Text is *qîqāyôn*, the name of some plant not yet identified with certainty. Modern dictionaries note that it is often identified with the castor-oil plant *(Ricinus communis)* but usually cite also the meanings given in the ancient versions.

4. *Ep.* 112.22; *CSEL* 55:392–93. In that letter, Jerome writes: "At the end of my letter, I ask that you do not force a retired old man and one already a veteran to do battle and to imperil his life again. You who are young and have been appointed to the episcopal dignity, teach the people and enrich the Roman house with new African crops. For me it is enough to whisper to some listener or reader in a poor little corner of a monastery."

5. "For the same Spirit who inspired the original Prophets as they wrote was no less present to the Seventy as they translated what the Prophets had written" (*De civ. Dei* 18.43; *CSEL* 40/2:337; Fathers of the Church 24:156).

6. *Ep.* 82.35; *CSEL* 34:396; tr. *Fathers of the Church* 12:419.

7. Luis Alonso Schökel, S.J., "Dove va l'esegesi cattolica?" *Civiltà Cattolica* 111, no. 2645 (3 September 1960) 449–60. The article also appeared in French, "Où va l'exégèse catholique?" *L'Ami du clergé* 71 (1961) 17–22. The French editors note: "For the permission to translate and publish these pages, we are grateful to the editorial board of the magazine *[Civ. Catt.]* and to the learned author, whose studied charity is united with a competence that our readers will recognize with pleasure."

8. *DaS* 11 (Béchard, SD, 121).

9. *DaS* 29 (Béchard, SD, 132).

10. *DaS* 25 (Béchard, SD 132); see pp. 33–34 below, where the text is quoted.

11. *AAS* 42 (1950) 561–78 (*EB* §§612–13; Béchard, SD, 140–41 [§§21–22]).

12. *Humani generis* 38 (EB §618; Béchard, *SD*, 143).

13. Antonino Romeo, "L'Enciclica '*Divino afflante Spiritu*' e le 'opiniones novae,'" *Divinitas* 4/3 (1960) 385–456.

14. Romeo mentions that Alonso Schökel was the author of some "aggressive" book reviews. Perhaps he is referring to the frank discussion written by Alonso Schökel of B. Mariani, *Introductio in libros sacros Veteris Testamenti* (Rome: Herder, 1958), reviewed in *Bib* 39 (1958) 499–502; *VDom* 36 (1958) 116–17. In substantial agreement with Alonso Schökel were many other Catholic reviewers: see "Elenchus bibliographicus biblicus" in *Bib* 41 (1960) 4*; *Razon y fe* 161 (1960) 367–80. Perhaps even more pertinent would be Alonso Schökel's review of F. Spadafora, A. Romeo, and D. Fragipane, *Il libro sacro 1: Introduzione generale* (Padua: Mesaggero, 1958), in which he says of Romeo's contribution on biblical inspiration: "I cannot recommend the treatise on inspiration to either lay people or students because of its polemics against Catholics who think differently" (*VDom* 38 [1960] 310).

15. See A. Vögtle, "Messiasbekenntnis und Petrusverheissung: Zur Komposition von Mt 16, 13–23," *BZ* 1 (1957) 252–72; 2 (1958) 85–103; P. Benoit, "La mort de Judas," *Synoptische Studien Alfred Wikenhauser zum siebzigsten Geburtstag...* (Munich: Zink, 1953) 1–19; A. Descamps, "La structure des récits évangeliques de la résurrection," *Bib* 40 (1959) 726–41. The summary character of Zerwick's address is, however, passed over in silence by Romeo. The president of the Italian Biblical Association thought it wise to issue certain clarifications about the Padua meeting, which could be consulted: "Clarificazioni sul Convegno di Padova (a proposito di un recente articolo) a cura del Presidente dell'Associazione," Appendix to the volume *Atti e Conferenze della Settimana Biblica 1960* (Rome, 1961).

16. Museum Lessianum, section biblique 1; Paris/Louvain: Desclée de Brouwer, 1958. That book was acclaimed widely by reviewers (*TS* 20 [1959] 282–84: "Without a doubt we have here one of the finest works on Scripture to appear in the last ten years" [J. E. Bruns]; *CBQ* 21 [1959] 245–47: "If this reviewer were asked to recommend a book which would give a thorough understanding of the present state of Catholic scholarship, he would unhesitatingly recommend this one" [L. A. Bushinski]; cf. similar reviews in *Angelicum* 36 [1959] 449; *ETL* 35 [1959] 824; *Bib* 40 [1959] 1025; *NTA* 4 [1959] 83–84; for a laudatory non-Catholic reaction, see *JBL* 79 [1960] 173–75). It was translated into English: *The Bible, Word of God in Words of Men* (New York: Kenedy, 1962).

17. Lyonnet, who was also a professor at the Biblical Institute, faced a milder form of criticism in the same magazine. His interpretation of Pauline teaching on original sin in Rom 5:12 (see "Le péché originel et l'exégese de Rom. 5, 12–14," *RSR* 44 [1956] 63–84; "Le sens de *eph' hô* en Rom 5, 12 et

l'exegese des Pères grecs," *Bib* 36 [1955] 436–56) was scrutinized by F. Spadafora ("Rom. 5, 12: Esegesi e riflessi dogmatici," *Divinitas* 4 [1960] 289–98) and judged "scientificamente infondata, per non dire insostenibile" (scientifically without foundation, not to mention untenable [p. 298]). See also B. Mariani, "La persona di Adamo e ii peccato originale secondo San Paolo: Rom. 5, 12–21," *Divinitas* 2 (1958) 486–519.

18. Oxford: Clarendon, 1951: "The Old Testament and the Archaeology of Palestine" (pp. 1–26); "The Old Testament and the Archaeology of the Ancient Near East" (pp. 27–47). In Italian dress, they appear under one title, "La Bibbia illustrata dall'archeologia," *Divinitas* 4 (1960) 457–505.

19. "Instituti fine continetur ut sanam de Libris sacris doctrinam, normis ab hac S. Sede Apostolica statutis vel statuendis omnino conformem, *adversus opiniones, recentiorum maxime, falsas, erroneas, temerarias atque haereticas defendat promulget, promoveat* (AAS 1 [1909] 448 [emphasis added by Romeo!]). (The purpose of the Institute is to defend, promulgate, and promote sound teaching about the Sacred Books, in thorough conformity with the norms set up or to be set up by this Holy Apostolic See, against opinions, especially of more recent [writers], which are false, erroneous, rash, and heretical.)

20. "Pontificium Institutum Biblicum et recens libellum R.mi D.ni A. Romeo," *VDom* 39 (1961) 3–17.

21. Ibid., 3–4.

22. I do not make public the text of the last two documents, since I have no authority to do so; though they were *not published* in Rome, they have been circulated widely. See further "The Close of a Controversy," *CBQ* 23 (1961) 269 and the references given there.

23. J. M. Le Blond, "L'Eglise et l'histoire," *Études* 309/1 (1961) 85–88.

24. E. Galbiati, "Un dissidio tra gli esegeti? A proposito di una recente polemica," *Scuola Cattolica* 89 (1961) 50–53, esp. 53.

25. See A. M[iller], "Das neue biblische Handbuch," *Benediktinische Monatschrift* [Beuron] 31 (1955) 49–50; A. Kleinhans, "De nova Enchiridii Biblici editione," *Antonianum* 30 (1955) 63–65. Cf. E. F. Siegman, "The Decrees of the Pontifical Biblical Commission: A Recent Clarification," *CBQ* 18 (1956) 23–29; J. Dupont, "A propos du nouvel Enchiridion Biblicum," *RB* 62 (1955) 414–19; B. Malina, "The Biblical Movement and the Decrees of the Biblical Commission," *Clergy Review* 46 (1961) 399–405.

This was an important issue, but it too was twisted and exploited by ultra-conservative interpreters. The message of the Secretary (A. Miller) and the Under-Secretary (A. Kleinhans), which was almost word-for-word the same despite the difference of languages (German and Latin) in which they wrote: "As long as these [early twentieth-century] decrees [of the Biblical Commission] propose views that are neither immediately nor mediately connected with truths of faith and morals, it goes without saying that the interpreter of Sacred Scripture may pursue his scientific research with complete freedom and utilize the results of these investigations, provided always that he respects the teaching authority of the Church" (Béchard, *SD*, 327). Most of the early *responsa* had nothing to do with "truths of faith and morals," but dealt with historical and literary judgments (e.g., Moses as author of the Pentateuch, the apostle John as the author of the Fourth Gospel). If modern scientific investigations conclude to "results" other than the *responsa*, the interpreter may adopt those "with complete freedom" *(mit aller Freiheit; plena libertate)*. The booklet, *Rome and the Study of Scripture* (7th ed.; St. Meinrad, IN: Grail Publications, 1962), however, twisted the meaning of this semi-official explanation by omitting the phrase, "with complete freedom" in its version of the explanation (note the omission on p. 175).

26. J. Lebreton, "Le désaccord de la foi populaire et de la théologie savante dans l'église chrétienne du IIIe siècle," *RHE* 19 (1923) 481–506; 20 (1924) 5–37.

27. Béchard, *SD*, 132.

28. *AAS* 53 (1961) 507 (Béchard, *SD*, 225).

29. A. Bea, *De Scripturae Sacrae Inspiratione* (2nd ed.; Rome: Biblical Institute, 1935) 106 §90.

Chapter Three: The Biblical Commission's Instruction on the Historical Truth of the Gospels

1. *ASS* 35 (1902–3) 234–38 (*EB* §§137–48; Béchard, *SD*, 62–66).

2. The Instruction was published in Latin on 14 May 1964 in *Osservatore Romano* p. 3 (with an Italian translation of the same); it also appeared in *AAS* 56 (1964) 712–18, where it bears the date 21 April 1964. An English translation of it appeared in Catholic newspapers in the U.S.A., but that translation was faulty in places and unreliable in the crucial paragraphs. I commented on the Instruction and appended an improved English translation of the Latin text of the *Osservatore Romano*, which preserved the paragraphs of the original (*TS* 25 [1964] 386–408). Only certain paragraphs in the Latin text were numbered with Arabic numerals. In order to facilitate references to the text, I added (capitalized) Roman numerals to all the paragraphs of the Instruction (preserving the Arabic numbers, where they were found). When my article with the translation was already in press, the secretary of the Biblical Commission issued an official English translation of the Instruction, which can be found in the *CBQ* 26 (1964) 305–12; or the *Tablet* [London] 218 (30 May 1964) 617–19. I continue to use my own translation of the Instruction (see pp.

50–57 below), which differs a little in wording from the official one (the latter can be found in Béchard, *SD*, 227–35 [where it too has added Roman numerals]).

3. The name of the Holy Office was changed later to the Congregation of the Doctrine of the Faith. Its *monitum* appeared in *AAS* 53 (1961) 507 (Béchard, *SD*, 225). For a translation of the full text of the *monitum*, see p. 34 above.

4. For the reaction of a non-Catholic interpreter to the Instruction, see F. W. Beare, "The Historical Truth of the Gospels: An Official Pronouncement of the Pontifical Biblical Commission," *Canadian Journal of Theology* 11 (1965) 231–37.

5. *The New York Times*, 14 May 1964, p. 37: "Vatican Cautions Students of Bible: Rejects as Dangerous and Invalid Any Conclusions Not Arising from Faith: Inquiry Limits Defined: Modern Historical Methods Accepted If Scholars Are Wary of 'Prejudices" (by Robert C. Doty). — *New York Herald Tribune*, 14 May 1964, p. 7: "Vatican Green Light to Bible Scholars" (by Sanche de Gramont).

6. Recall the end of n. 2 above (about the added Roman numerals used in references).

7. This sentence echoed the words of the 1961 *monitum* of the Holy Office, but what is significant is the simpler phraseology that has been introduced. The *monitum* had complained about opinions and views that were circulating, "that call into question the genuine historical and objective truth of Sacred Scripture — not only of the Old Testament...but also of the New Testament, and even with regard to the words and actions of Jesus Christ.

8. The Latin text reads: "Alii e falsa notione fidei procedunt ac si ipsa veritatem historicam non curet, immo cum eadem componi non possit" (Others begin with a false idea of faith, as if it had nothing to do with historical truth — or rather were incompatible with it) (par. V). — The immediately following sentence uses the phrase "historicam vim et indolem documentorum revelationis" (the historical value and nature of documents of revelation), an expression that has a wider connotation.

9. The italics of the original text have been reproduced in my translation, so that the structure of the Instruction would be evident. The principle governing the use of Arabic numerals for certain paragraphs changes after a while, so that they are not a real guide to the structure of the document.

10. As in the case of the *responsa* and other instructions of the Biblical Commission, this document is not considered to be infallible (in the technical sense). — The *Motu Proprio* of Pope Pius X on the decisions of the Biblical Commission, *Praestantia Sacrae Scripturae* (ASS 40 [1907] 723–26; *EB* §§96–98; Béchard, *SD*, 78–79), declared that such decisions "have proved very

useful for the promotion and guidance of sound biblical scholarship in accordance with the established norms." That formulated their utilitarian and practical aim or purpose. However, Pius X added: "all are bound in conscience to submit to the decisions of the Biblical Commission, which have been given in the past and shall be given in the future, *in the same way as the Decrees pertaining to doctrine issued by the Sacred Congregations and approved by the Sovereign Pontiff* (emphasis of the original). That statement of Pius X was reiterated in the Commission's *Responsum* of 27 February 1934 (*EB* §519). Debate ensued among theologians whether the decisions of the Biblical Commission were disciplinary or doctrinal; most seemed to think that they were not merely disciplinary, but indirectly doctrinal. There was also a discussion whether they were concerned with *veritas* (truth) or *securitas*. Cf. L. Pirot, "Commission biblique," *DBSup* 2:111–13. For a later semi-official clarification of the value of the Commission's "decrees" *(responsa)*, see E. F. Siegman, "The Decrees of the Pontifical Biblical Commission," *CBQ* 18 (1956) 23–29; see n. 25 on p. 120–21.

11. The outspoken opponent of the study of literary forms of the Bible, E. Cardinal Ruffini, was himself a member of the Biblical Commission that then publicly reiterated Pius XII's injunction to exegetes of the Church to pursue such study, especially with regard to the Gospels. Cardinal Ruffini's rejection of this type of study was made in his article "Generi letterari e ipotesi di lavoro nei recenti studi biblici," *Osservatore Romano* 24 August 1961, p. 1. Appearing on the front page of such a prominent organ, and having been sent by the Sacred Congregation of Studies and Universities to the rectors of all Italian seminaries, it was accorded no little respect. It appeared in an English translation in many American Catholic newspapers; see "Literary Genres and Working Hypotheses in Recent Biblical Studies," *AER* 145 (1961) 362–65. In that article, Cardinal Ruffini went so far in his disagreement as to quote Pius XII indirectly and to use the word "absurdity" to describe the study of these forms. The 1964 Instruction put an end to the confusion that his article had created.

12. For a brief discussion of the problems involved, see R. E. Brown, *An Introduction to the New Testament* (ABRL; New York: Doubleday, 1997) 22–23; W. G. Kümmel, *Introduction to the New Testament* (Nashville, TN: Abingdon, 1975) 10–12, 75–78; A. Wikenauser, *New Testament Introduction* (New York: Herder & Herder, 1958) 253–77; A. Wikenhauser and J. Schmid, *Einleitung in das Neue Testament* (6th ed.; Freiburg im B.: Herder, 1973) 290–96.

13. The sixth item seems to have been directed against the pioneer German proponents of form criticism, whose ideas of *Gemeindetheologie* were rejected by many. Cf. V. T. O'Keefe, "Toward Understanding the Gospels," *CBQ* 21 (1959) 171–89.

There is a sense in which one can say legitimately that the early community "created" a story about Jesus. For instance, in the matter of divorce, the

Sitz im Leben may well have been either a debate or the solving of some specific case of conscience ("Do we Christians permit divorce or not?"). Words of Jesus on the subject would have been recalled, and thus the story was "created" at that time. Such a story was likely to have been repeated until it became a norm for deciding cases. In such a form, it may well have been passed through the early Church (or Churches) for a generation, until it became part of the gospel tradition. The difficulty with the verb "created," however, is that it often connotes fabrication from the whole cloth. Perhaps it would be better to speak of the "formation" of the story in the early Church, rather than its "creation."

14. C. H. Dodd, *The Apostolic Preaching and Its Developments* (London: Hodder & Stoughton, 1944; repr., New York: Harper, 1962).

15. The Latin word is *narrationes*, which some may prefer to translate as "narratives." In par. IX, it occurs in the singular in the sense of "account," because of its allusion to Luke 1:1. Neither "narrative" nor "account," however, sufficiently conveys the idea of a literary form, whereas "story" does. It may be objected that this word is "loaded," connoting "fable, fairy tale," etc. True, it often has such a connotation, but not always, and not necessarily. In the long run, the word "story" connotes what is factual. I am using the word "story" without implying any pejorative connotation or value judgment.

16. The Latin text of this sentence reads: "Cum ex eis quae novae inquisitiones contulerunt appareat doctrinam et vitam Jesu non simpliciter relatas fuisse, eo solo fine ut memoria tenerentur, sed 'praedicatas' fuisse ita ut Ecclesiae fundamentum fidei et morum praeberent, interpres testimonium Evangelistarum indefesse perscrutans, vim theologicam perennem Evangeliorum altius illustrare et quantae sit Ecclesiae interpretatio necessitatis quantique momenti in plena luce collocare valebit" (par. X).

17. The translation is from Béchard, *SD*, 132.

18. See chapter 2 above, "A Roman Scripture Controversy, pp. 17–36."

19. It is no secret that the first draft of the schema prepared for the Second Vatican Council, *De fontibus revelationis*, contained two paragraphs that incorporated the terminology of the 1961 *monitum* of the Holy Office. The draft leveled anathemas against those who would call in question the genuine historical and objective truth of the words and deeds of Jesus, as they are recounted *(prouti narrantur)*. That terminology was rejected, along with the rest of the schema, and the schema that replaced it, *De divina revelatione*, which eventually became the Dogmatic Constitution *Dei Verbum*, adopted a more proper approach to the topic. In fact, §19 of *Dei Verbum* echoed the teaching of this Instruction of the Biblical Commission. See p. 10 above.

20. Although the main directives of the Instruction (par. IV–XI) have been addressed to exegetes, dogmatic theologians and others, whose work is related to Scripture, will have to reckon also with the import of this document. We have

been told that "there exists a numerous and fairly articulate group convinced that the four Gospels and Acts of the Apostles are genuine and objectively accurate historical documents, which can be used as such legitimately in the science of apologetics. These individuals insist that they have reason to hold and to teach that these events set forth in these books took place in the very way in which they are described in these works. They hold that the words and the deeds attributed to Our Lord were actually uttered and performed by Him…" (J. C. Fenton, "Father Moran's Prediction," *AER* 146 [1962] 194–95). Such a position had to be nuanced, if not abandoned, in light of this Instruction of 1964!

21. Compare Luke's form, "Blessed are you poor," with Matthew's "Blessed are the poor in spirit"; Luke's "Blessed are you that hunger now," with Matthew's "Blessed are those who hunger and thirst for righteousness," etc. See the treatment of such differences by J. Dupont, *Les Beatitudes I* (Bruges: Abbaye de saint André, 1958), II (Etudes bibliques; Paris: Gabalda, 1969).

22. See R. E. Brown et al. (eds.), *Peter in the New Testament* (Minneapolis, MN: Augsburg; New York: Paulist, 1973) 83–101. Cf. A. Vögtle, "Messiasbekenntnis und Petrusverheissung: Zur Komposition Mt 16, 13–23 Par.," *BZ* 1 (1957) 252–72; 2 (1958) 85–102; E. F. Sutcliffe, "St. Peter's Double Confession in Mt. 16:16–19," *Heythrop Journal* 3 (1962) 31–41.

23. The Latin text reads, "Quaedam a multis traditis selegentes, quaedam in synthesim redigentes, quaedam ad statum ecclesiarum attendendo explanantes."

24. See P. Benoit, *L'Evangile selon saint Matthieu* (La Bible de Jérusalem; 3rd ed.; Paris: Cerf, 1961) 121; H. J. Richards, "Christ on Divorce," *Scripture* 11 (1959) 22–32; J. A. Fitzmyer, "The Matthean Divorce Texts and Some New Palestinian Evidence," *TS* 37 (1976) 197–226, esp. 207–11 (reprinted in *To Advance the Gospel: New Testament Studies* [New York: Crossroad, 1981] 79–111 [see esp. 87–89]).

25. See also the statement of the Second Vatican Council about the purpose of biblical inerrancy in *Dei Verbum* §11: "Since everything asserted by the inspired authors or sacred writers should be regarded as asserted by the Holy Spirit, it follows that we must acknowledge the Books of Scripture as teaching firmly, faithfully, and without error the truth that God wished to be recorded in the sacred writings for the sake of our salvation" (Béchard, *SD*, 24).

Chapter Four: Historical Criticism: Its Role in Biblical Interpretation and Church Life

1. See, e.g., L. Ayres and S. E. Fowl, "(Mis)reading the Face of God: *The Interpretation of the Bible in the Church*," *TS* 60 (1999) 513–28 (on which read

R. E. Murphy, "Quaestio Disputata: Is the Paschal Mystery the Primary Hermeneutic Principle?" *TS* 61 [2000] 139–46); M. Couve de Murville, "The Catholic Church and the Critical Study of the Bible," *Epworth Review* 13 (1986) 76–86; N. S. L. Fryer, "The Historical-Critical Method — Yes or No?" *Scripture* 20 (1987) 41–70; J. D. Levenson, *The Hebrew Bible the Old Testament and Historical Criticism: Jews and Christians in Biblical Studies* (Louisville, KY: Westminster John Knox, 1993); E. Linnemann, *Historical Criticism of the Bible: Methodology or Ideology?* (Grand Rapids, MI: Baker, 1990); G. Maier, *The End of the Historical-Critical Method* (St. Louis, MO: Concordia, 1974); P. Patterson and N. James, "The Historical-critical Study of the Bible: Dangerous or Helpful?" *Theological Educator* 37 (1988) 45–74; B. D. Smith, "The Historical-Critical Method, Jesus Research, and the Christian Scholar," *Trinity Journal* 15 (1994) 201–20.

2. A sociologist, Msgr. George A. Kelly, published a book entitled *The New Biblical Theorists: Raymond E. Brown and Beyond* (Ann Arbor, MI: Servant Books, 1983), in which he inveighed against the renowned Sulpician biblical scholar, who was a gifted practitioner of the method. (I was part of the "and beyond.") Cf. R. E. Brown, "Historical-Critical Exegesis and Attempts at Revisionism," *The Bible Today* 23 (1985) 157–65. See further chapter 7 below.

3. By J. Hitchcock, *U.S. National Catholic Register*.

4. *New York Review of Books*, 14 June 1984, 35–38. It was supposed to be a review of Hans Küng's book, *Eternal Life after Death as a Medical, Philosophical, and Theological Problem* (Garden City, NY: Doubleday, 1984), but Sheehan used the occasion to complain about those in the Church who were using the historical-critical method of interpretation and those who were exploiting their findings. Compare Sheehan's book, *The First Coming: How the Kingdom of God Became Christianity* (New York: Random House, 1986), but also the review of it by J. P. Galvin, *TS* 48 (1987) 739–41.

5. Sheehan, "Revolution," 35.

6. See J. Quasten, *Patrology* (3 vols.; Westminster, MD: Newman), 2 (1953) 44–45.

7. See R. F. Collins, "Augustine of Hippo: Precursor of Modern Biblical Scholarship," *Louvain Studies* 12 (1987) 131–51. Cf. J. N. D. Kelly, *Jerome: His Life Writings and Controversies* (London: Duckworth, 1976) passim.

8. More will be said about this sense in chapter 6 below.

9. See P. Stuhlmacher, *Historical Criticism and Theological Interpretation of Scripture* (Philadelphia, PA: Fortress, 1977) 32–36.

10. Leopold von Ranke, *Geschichte der romanischen und germanischen Völker bis 1514: Zur Kritik neuer Geschichtschreiber* (Sämmtliche Werke 33–34; 3rd ed.; Leipzig: Duncker & Humblot, 1865) vii ("er will bloss zeigen wie es eigentlich gewesen").

11. See C. H. Talbert (ed.), *Reimarus Fragments* (Lives of Jesus series; Philadelphia, PA: Fortress, 1970); H. S. Reimarus, *The Goal of Jesus and His Disciples* (ed. G. W. Buchanan; Leiden: Brill, 1970). Cf. the critique of Reimarus in D. F. Strauss, *Hermann Samuel Reimarus und seine Schutzschrift für die vernünftigen Verehrer Gottes* (Hildesheim/Zurich: Olms, 1991 [reprint of 1863 edition]).

12. For details about the discoveries and their impact, see pp. 4, 79–80.

13. Edition augmentée (Paris: Lecoffre, 1904); in English, *Historical Criticism and the Old Testament* (London: Catholic Truth Society, 1905).

14. See *AAS* 35 (1943) 297–325 (*EB* §§538–69; Béchard, *SD*, 115–36).

15. See further E. Krentz, *The Historical-Critical Method* (Guides to Biblical Scholarship; Philadelphia, PA: Fortress, 1975).

16. See D. Robertson, "Literature, the Bible as," *IDBSup* 547–51. "These scholars, who come from diverse philosophical and theological traditions, are united in considering the Bible primarily and fundamentally as a literary document (as opposed, e.g., to considering it as a historical or theological document)" (p. 547).

In this regard, it might be good to quote an assessment of the literary criticism of the Bible once penned by T. S. Eliot: "While I acknowledge the legitimacy of this enjoyment, I am acutely aware of its abuse. The persons who enjoy these writings *solely* because of their literary merit are essentially parasites; and we know that parasites, when they become too numerous, are pests. I could fulminate against the men of letters who have gone into ecstacies over 'the Bible as literature,' the Bible as 'the noblest monument of English prose.' Those who talk of the Bible as a 'monument of English prose' are merely admiring it as a monument over the grave of Christianity. I must try to avoid the by-paths of my discourse; it is enough to suggest that just as the work of Clarendon, or Gibbon, or Buffon, or Bradley would be of inferior literary value if it were insignificant as history, science and philosophy respectively, so the Bible has had a *literary* influence upon English literature *not* because it has been considered as literature, but because it has been considered as the report of the Word of God. And the fact that men of letters now discuss it as 'literature' probably indicates the end of its 'literary' influence" (*Selected Essays: New Edition* [New York: Harcourt, Brace, 1950] 344–45).

17. As Cardinal A. Bea once put it, "Sua cuique generi literario est veritas" (Each literary form has its own truth); see *De sacrae Scripturae inspiratione* (2nd ed.; Rome: Biblical Institute, 1935) 106 §90.

18. See further the discussion of these stages in chapter 3 above.

19. See C. Hartlich, "Is Historical Criticism out of Date?" in *Conflicting Ways of Interpreting the Bible* (Concilium 138; ed. H. Küng and J. Moltmann; New York: Seabury, 1980) 3–8.

20. Albert Schweitzer, *The Quest of the Historical Jesus: A Critical Study of Its Progress from Reimarus to Wrede* (London: Black, 1910; repr., 1948) 4–5.

21. R. Bultmann, *History of the Synoptic Tradition* (Oxford: Blackwell, 1963) 11–69. M. Dibelius (*From Tradition to Gospel* [New York: Scribner, 1935] 40–43) called it a "paradigm," whereas V. Taylor (*Formation of the Gospel Tradition* [London: Macmillan, 1949130]) more accurately labelled it a "pronouncement story," i.e., a narrative account that enshrines a punch-line saying of Jesus.

22. R. Bultmann, *Theology of the New Testament 1* (London: SCM, 1952) 3. See also Bultmann's *Jesus and the Word* (New York: Scribner, 1958); *Jesus Christ and Mythology* (New York: Scribner, 1958).

23. See further J. Macquarrie, *An Existentialist Theology: A Comparison of Heidegger and Bultmann* (New York: Macmillan, 1955). Cf. B. Jaspert, *Rudolf Bultmanns Werk und Wirkung* (Darmstadt: Wissenschaftliche Buchgesellschaft, 1984); C. W. Kegley, *The Theology of Rudolf Bultmann* (London: SCM, 1966); N. Perrin, *The Promise of Bultmann* (Philadelphia, PA: Fortress, 1969).

24. See further J. Ratzinger, "Foundations and Approaches of Biblical Exegesis," *Origins* 17/35 (11 February 1988) 593–602. The same article was published under the title, "Biblical Interpretation in Crisis: On the Question of the Foundations and Approaches of Exegesis Today," *This World* 22 (1988) 3–19.

25. See R. W. Funk et al., *The Five Gospels: The Search for the Authentic Words of Jesus* (San Francisco, CA: HarperSanFrancisco, 1993); *The Acts of Jesus: The Search for the Authentic Deeds of Jesus* (San Francisco, CA: HarperSanFrancisco, 1998). Cf. L. T. Johnson, *The Misguided Quest for the Historical Jesus and the Truth of the Traditional Gospels* (San Francisco, CA: HarperSanFrancisco, 1997).

26. See his article "Ist voraussetzungslose Exegese möglich?" *TZ* 13 (1957) 409–17; reprinted in his *Glauben und Verstehen: Gesammelte Aufsätze III* (Tübingen: Mohr [Siebeck], 1960) 142–50; in English, "Is Exegesis without Presuppositions Possible?" in *Existence and Faith: Shorter Writings of Rudolf Bultmann* (ed. S. M. Ogden; London: Hodder & Stoughton, 1960) 289–96.

27. See further H. Cazelles, "Anwendung und Erfahrungen mit der historisch-kritischen Methode in der katholischen Exegese," in *Der historisch-kritische Methode und die heutige Suche nach einem lebendigen Verständnis der Bibel* (ed. H. Riedlinger; Freiburg im B.: Katholische Akademie; Munich: Schnell & Steiner, 1985) 72–88; but beware of what D. Farkasfalvy calls a "'post-critical' method" in his article, "In search of a 'post-critical' method of biblical interpretation for Catholic theology," *International Catholic Review/Communio* 13 (1986) 288–307. Some of the approaches he singles

out are found among those mentioned above as refinements or correctives of the basic method.

28. *DaS* 22 (Béchard, *SD*, 130).

29. *DaS* 15 (Béchard, *SD*, 125). The words are quoted on p. 87.

30. *DaS* 15 (Béchard, *SD*, 125).

31. *DaS* 16 (Béchard, *SD*, 125).

32. An English translation of the full text of the Instruction, along with a commentary on it, can be found in chapter 3, pp. 37–58.

33. *Dei Verbum* §19 (Béchard, *SD*, 27–28); §19 begins with "Holy Mother Church," using the same words with which the Biblical Commission's Instruction begins.

See further J. Dupont, "Storicità dei vangeli e metodo storico dell'esegesi nella constituzione dogmatica 'Dei Verbum,'" in *A venti anni dal Concilio: Prospettive teologiche e giuridiche: Atti del convegno di studi "Il Concilio Vaticano II venti anni dopo" Catania 21–22 aprile 5–6 maggio 1983* (Palermo: Edizioni 0 F Te S, 1984) 51–73. Cf. J. Gnilka, "Die biblische Exegese im Lichte des Dekretes über die göttliche Offenbarung *(Dei Verbum),*" *Münchener theologische Zeitschrift* 36 (1985) 5–19.

34. The text was issued only in French (the original language) and Latin (on facing pages): *Bible et christologie* (ed. H. Cazelles; Paris: Cerf, 1984) 13–109. An English translation of it can be found in my article "The Biblical Commission and Christology," *TS* 46 (1985) 407–79, esp. 408–43; and in my book *Scripture and Christology: A Statement of the Biblical Commission with a Commentary* (New York/Mahwah, NJ: Paulist, 1986) 3–53.

35. See further E. Zenger, "Von der Unverzichtbarkeit der historisch-kritischen Exegese: Am Beispiel des 46. Psalms," *Bibel und Liturgie* 62 (1989) 10–20. — It is worth noting that this sort of critical reading has been extended from the Bible to teachings of the Church's magisterium itself. Thus *Mysterium ecclesiae* (AAS 65 [1973] 116–17; DH 4539) admitted the need to recognize the historical, time-conditioned character of Church pronouncements: though the Church can teach infallibly, its exposition of revelation may involve language of a given time, may be expressed at first incompletely, may be limited in character, and may involve conceptions of a given period.

36. See further R. E. Brown, "The Contribution of Historical Biblical Criticism to Ecumenical Church Discussion," in R. J. Neuhaus (ed.), *Biblical Interpretation in Crisis: The Ratzinger Conference on Bible and Church* (Encounter Series 9; Grand Rapids, MI: Eerdmans, 1989) 24–49; drastically abbreviated in a German translation in J. Ratzinger (ed.), *Schriftauslegung im Widerstreit* (QD 117; Freiburg im B.: Herder, 1989) 81–97. Cf. T. R. Curtin, *Historical Criticism and the Theological Interpretation of Scripture: The*

Catholic Discussion of a Biblical Hermeneutic 1958–1983 (Rome: Gregorian University, 1987).

Chapter Five: Concerning the Interpretation of the Bible in the Church

1. P. R. Davies, *Whose Bible Is It Anyway?* (JSOTSup 204; Sheffield, UK: Sheffield Academic Press, 1995).
2. Ibid., 4.
3. Ibid., 11–12.
4. Ibid., 12.
5. Ibid., 13.
6. Ibid., 14.
7. Ibid., 15.
8. Ibid., 16.
9. Ibid., 15 (his italics).
10. Ibid.
11. Ibid., 16.
12. In saying this, I do not agree with the views of P. Perkins, "The New Testament — the Church's Book??!," *Proceedings of the Catholic Theological Society of America* 40 (1985) 36–53. See the response of J. A. Sanders to her views (ibid., 54–63).
13. I am using "Bible" here in the Christian sense as the OT and the NT. For a Jew, the answer would be: the Hebrew Scriptures belong to the Jewish people, to God's Chosen People in the pre-Christian age and to their counterparts today.
14. In other words, the first and second parts of the Hebrew Scriptures according to the way Jewish people normally have divided their sacred writings: *Tôrāh, Nĕbî'îm, and Kĕtûbîm,* "Law, Prophets, and Writings," abbreviated as *Tĕnāk.*
15. See the rule books of the Qumran community (1QS 1:3; cf. 1QS 8:15; CD 5:21–6:1), which use the same phrase.
16. Recall the words of T. S. Eliot quoted above on p. 127 n. 16, who is cited by Davies as a representative of "non-confessional interpretation" (*Whose Bible*, 13–14).
17. See *L'Interprétation de la Bible dans l'Église.* The details about this publication have already been given in chapter 1, n. 23 (p. 117 above). Quotations in this essay are drawn from the Vatican's English form (*The Interpretation*) and reference to my book will be added as "JAF, *Text.*"
18. *The Interpretation,* 30–31; JAF, *Text,* 19.

19. *The Interpretation*, 34; JAF, *Text*, 26.

20. The *Interpretation*, 34; JAF, *Text*, 27–31. See further pp. 61–62 above.

21. See E. A. Wallis Budge, *The Rosetta Stone in the British Museum* (London: Religious Tract Society, 1929); idem, *The Decrees of Memphis and Canopus* (New York: Frowde, 1904); R. Lepsius, *Der bilingue Dekret von Kanopus: In der Originalgrosse mit Übersetzung und Erklärung beider Texte* (Berlin: Hertz, 1866); C. Andrews, *The British Museum Book of the Rosetta Stone* (New York: Dorset, 1981); C. Lagier, *Autour de la pierre de Rosette* (Brussels: Fondation Egyptologique Reine Elisabeth, 1927).

22. See, e.g., J. Assmann et al., "Egyptian Literature," ABD 2:378–99. Cf. J. B. Pritchard (ed.), *The Ancient Near Eastern Texts Relating to the Old Testament* (3rd ed.; Princeton, NJ: Princeton University Press, 1969); idem, *The Ancient Near East: Supplementary Texts and Pictures Relating to the Old Testament* (Princeton, NJ: Princeton University Press, 1969) passim.

23. Also called Behistun or Bisutun Stone.

24. See H. C. Rawlinson, *The Persian Cuneiform Inscription at Behistun* (London: J. W. Parker, 1846). Cf. E. Hincks, *On the First and Second Kinds of Persepolitan Writing* (Dublin: Gill, 1846); L. W. King and R. C. Thomson, *The Sculptures and Inscription of Darius the Great on the Rock of Behistun in Persia* (London: British Museum, 1907). An Aramaic translation of this inscription was found at Elephantine, Egypt, in the early part of the twentieth century; see J. C. Greenfield and B. Porten, *The Bisitun Inscription of Darius the Great: Aramaic Version* (Corpus inscriptionum iranicarum, ser. 15; London: Lund Humphries, 1982).

25. See, e.g., A. K. Grayson, "Mesopotamia, History of, "ABD 4:732–77. Cf. Pritchard, *Ancient Near Eastern Texts*, passim; B. R. Foster, *Before the Muses: An Anthology of Akkadian Literature* (2 vols.; Bethesda, MD: CDL Press, 1993); W. W. Hallo et al. (eds.), *The Bible in the Light of Cuneiform Literature* (Ancient Near Eastern Texts and Studies 8; Lewiston, NY/Queenstown, ON/Lampeter, Wales: Edwin Mellen, 1990).

26. See A. Deissmann, *Light from the Ancient East: The New Testament Illustrated by Recently Discovered Texts of the Graeco-Roman World* (2nd ed.; London: Hodder & Stoughton; New York: Doran, 1927).

27. See D. Pardee and P. Bordreuil, "Ugarit: Texts and Literature," ABD 6:706–21; N. Wyatt, *Religious Texts from Ugarit: The Words of Ilimilku and His Colleagues* (Sheffield, UK: Sheffield Academic Press, 1998); W. van der Meer and J. C. de Moor, *The Structural Analysis of Biblical and Canaanite Poetry* (JSOTSup 74; Sheffield, UK: Sheffield Academic Press, 1988); M. S. Smith, *Untold Stories: The Bible and Ugaritic Studies in the Twentieth Century* (Peabody, MA: Hendrickson, 2001).

28. See F. García Martínez and W. G. E. Watson, *The Dead Sea Scrolls Translated: The Qumran Texts in English* (2nd ed.; Leiden: Brill; Grand Rapids, MI: Eerdmans, 1996). Cf. J. A. Fitzmyer, *Responses to 101 Questions on the Dead Sea Scrolls* (New York: Paulist Press, 1992) 104–41; G. Vermes, *The Dead Sea Scrolls: Qumran in Perspective* (rev. ed.; Philadelphia, PA: Fortress, 1977).

29. ASS 26 (1893–94) 269–92 (DH 3280–94; *EB* §§81–134; Béchard, *SD*, 37–61).

30. AAS 12 (1920) 385–422 (DH 3650–54; *EB* §§440–95; Béchard, *SD* 81–111, esp. 90 [§7: where *genera...litterarum* is poorly translated as "kinds of literature" instead of "literary genres"]).

31. See Béchard, *SD*, 115–39, especially 128–29 (§20).

32. These approaches are treated in section 1:B of the Commission's document, *The Interpretation*, 41–50; cf. JAF, *Text*, 50–67.

33. See *The Interpretation*, 69–72; cf. JAF, *Text*, 101–8. The English translation entitles section I:F as "Fundamentalist Interpretation," whereas the original French version has as the title "Lecture fondamentaliste," a title that was chosen expressly by the Commission in order not to grace such a mode of "reading" with the status of a method or approach.

34. See D. Bergant, "Fundamentalism and the Biblical Commission," *Chicago Studies* 34 (1995) 209–21; E. Discherl, "Pluralität ja — Fundamentalismus nein! Vom Umgang mit der Bibel in 'postmodernen' Zeiten," *Bibel und Liturgie* 70 (1997) 208–12; W. Gross, "Rom gegen den Fundamentalismus," *Theologische Quartalschrift* 174 (1994) 232–34; S. B. Marrow, *The Words of Jesus: A Catholic Response to Fundamentalism* (New York: Paulist, 1979); A. Schenker, "Der biblische Fundamentalismus und die katholische Kirche," *Internationale Katholische Zeitschrift/Communio* 30 (2001) 507–12; J. C. de Smidt, "Fundamentalism — Historical Survey," *Scriptura* 64 (1998) 37–49.

35. Vatican Council II, *Dei Verbum* (Dogmatic Constitution on Divine Revelation) 12 (Béchard, *SD*, 28 [§21]).

36. These words are not taken from *Dei Verbum* but are my translation of what L. Bouyer wrote in "Liturgie et exégèse spirituelle," *La Maison Dieu* 7 (1946) 27–50, esp. 30. He used them of what he wanted to call (wrongly) the "spiritual" sense; they express rather the literal sense itself and its actualization.

37. *The Interpretation*, 113–17; cf. JAF, *Text*, 170–76.

38. *The Interpretation*, 113; cf. JAF, *Text*, 171. See also M. Dumais, "L'Actualisation de l'Ecriture: Fondements et procédures," *Science et Esprit* 51 (1999) 27–47.

39. As P. Williamson has maintained (mistakenly) in an article, "Actualization: A New Emphasis in Catholic Scripture Study," *America* 172 (20 May 1995) 17–19, esp. 19.

40. As an example of the way the Epistle to the Romans may be used as a source of genuine Christian spirituality, see J. A. Fitzmyer, *Spiritual Exercises Based on Paul's Epistle to the Romans* (Grand Rapids, MI: Eerdmans, 2004).

Chapter Six: The Senses of Scripture

1. See J. A. Fitzmyer, "The Use of Explicit Old Testament Quotations in Qumran Literature and in the New Testament," *ESBNT* or *SBNT*, 3–58, where one will find a discussion of different ways of interpreting the OT.

2. See also Luke 24:25–27; Acts 13:29; John 12:16; 20:9.

3. See J. K. Elliott, *The Apocryphal New Testament: A Collection of Apocryphal Christian Literature in an English Translation* (Oxford: Clarendon, 1993) 142.

4. See A. T. Hanson, *Jesus Christ in the Old Testament* (London: SPCK, 1965); R. H. Judd, *Jesus Christ in the Old Testament* (Oregon, IL: National Bible Institution, 1928).

5. See further M. Hasitschka, "Wörtlicher und geistlicher Sinn der Schrift," *Bibel und Liturgie* 70 (1997) 152–55.

6. See R. E. Brown, "Hermeneutics," *NJBC*, 1148 (§9); also his book, *An Introduction to the New Testament* (ABRL; New York: Doubleday, 1997) 35–36.

7. *AAS* 35 (1943) 310 (*EB* §550; Béchard, *SD*, 125 [§15]).

8. *Summa Theologiae* I q. 1, a. 10 ("Sensus literalis est, quem auctor intendit"); cf. *Quaestiones Quodlibetales* VII q. 16, a. 14–16.

9. *S.T.* I q. 1, a. 10 ad 2.

10. *S.T.* I q. 1, a. 10 ad 3.

11. *S.T.* I q. 1, a.9.

12. *The Interpretation*, 79; cf. JAF, *Text*, 120–21.

13. Ibid., 78–79.

14. "Directly" would have to be understood as it is explained in the first paragraph of this section. Avery Cardinal Dulles has suggested that "directly" would mean "intentionally" or "consciously" ("The Interpretation of the Bible in the Church: A Theological Appraisal," in *Kirche sein: Nachkonziliare Theologie im Dienst der Kirchenreform: Für Hermann Josef Pottmeyer* [Freiburg im B.: Herder, 1994] 29–37, esp. 31). Such a meaning of "directly" was not in the minds of the members of the Commission, of which I was one; in fact, it was excluded.

15. See, e.g., N. Watson, "Authorial Intention: Suspect Concept for Bible Scholarship," *Australian Biblical Review* 15 (1987) 6–13.

16. *The Interpretation*, 80; cf. JAF, *Text*, 122–23.

17. *The Interpretation*, 79; cf. JAF, *Text*, 122.

18. *The Interpretation*, 79; cf. JAF, *Text*, 122.

19. See *DaS* 25–26 (*EB* §552; Béchard, *SD*, 125–26 [§16]).

20. *The Interpretation*, 81; cf. JAF, *Text*, 127–28.

21. See further P. Grelot, *Sens chrétien de l'Ancien Testament* (Tournai: Desclée, 1962) 442–99; P. Beauchamp, "Lecture christique de l'Ancien Testament," *Bib* 81 (2000) 105–15; V. Balaguer, "El sentido literal y el sentido espiritual de la Sagrada Escritura," *Scripta theologica* [Pamplona] 36 (2004) 509–63.

22. See further L. Bouyer, *The Meaning of Sacred Scripture* (Liturgical Studies; Notre Dame, IN: University of Notre Dame, 1958) 227–28; A. Dulles, *The Craft of Theology: From Symbol to System* (New York: Crossroad, 1992) 69–85, esp. 73–76.

23. *Peri Archōn* 4.3.5 (GCS 22:331; SC 268:362). Cf. H. de Lubac, *Histoire et Esprit: L'Intelligence de l'Ecriture d'après Origène* (Paris: Aubier, 1950) 92–194; H. Crouzel, *Origen* (San Francisco, CA: Harper & Row, 1989) 61–84.

24. See further H. de Lubac, *The Sources of Revelation* (New York: Herder and Herder, 1968) 13.

25. *The Interpretation*, 97; cf. JAF, *Text*, 150.

26. Ibid.

27. *The Interpretation*, 82; cf. JAF, *Text*, 128–29.

28. *The Interpretation*, 82; cf. JAF, *Text*, 127.

29. As quoted in Nicholas of Lyra, *Postilla in Gal.* 4.3, the last clause reads rather *quo tendas anagogia*. The distich is ascribed usually to Augustine of Dacia, O.P., who was of Scandinavian origin (d. 1282); but it merely formulated what was distinguished earlier in the time of Augustine of Hippo.

30. *S.T.* I q. 1, a. 10: "Illa ergo prima significatio, qua voces significant res, pertinet ad primum sensum, qui est sensus historicus vel literalis."

31. *The Interpretation*, 82; cf. JAF, *Text*, 127.

32. Paul once wrote that the minds of the Jewish people of old "were dulled, to this very day, when the old covenant is read the veil remains unlifted; it is only in Christ that it is taken away" (2 Cor 3:14). That, of course, is a christological way of reading Moses. "Only in Christ" is the added (Christian) spiritual meaning given by Paul to the words of Moses.

33. Dulles, "The Interpretation" (n. 14 above), 31–32. Dulles also finds it difficult to accept the Commission's view of the Tridentine interpretation of Rom 5:12 in terms of original sin as an adequate example of the *sensus plenior*.

For him "the language of the Council seems to indicate an intention to inter-pret Paul's literal meaning" (p. 32). And yet Dulles grants that "Trent is admit-tedly dealing with a point slightly different from what Paul had in mind, and is relying in part on the Vulgate translation of Rom 5:12, which read: '...in whom [Adam] all have sinned' *(in quo omnes peccaverunt)*. But it seems clear that the Council was intending to interpret the thought of Paul himself." But if the "point" is "slightly different from what Paul has in mind," is there not room for a *sensus plenior,* which the Tradition that Trent was enshrining officially has made known? After all, in the sixteenth century no one ever spoke of a "fuller sense," a notion that has come into Catholic discussion of the senses of Scripture only in the twentieth century. It has proved to be a notion that allows one today to understand more properly the kind of definition in which the Council of Trent was engaged. I find it difficult to think that the Council defined that *peccatum originale,* a Western, Latin theological concept, which is lacking in the Eastern, Greek patristic Tradition, is the "literal sense" of Rom 5:12. Cf. my discussion of this point in *Scripture, the Soul of Theology* (New York/Mahwah, NJ: Paulist, 1994) 69, esp. n. 21; and in *Romans* (AB 33; New York: Doubleday, 1993) 409–10.

34. See his *Institutiones Biblicae* (Rome: Biblical Institute, 1925; 2nd ed., 1927) 305–7. Also his articles, "Sensus typicus, *sensus plenior,*" *Bib* 33 (1952) 526–28; "Sentido plenior, literal, típico, espiritual," *Bib* 34 (1953) 299–326. Cf. R. E. Brown, *The* Sensus plenior *of Sacred Scripture* (Baltimore, MD: St. Mary's University, 1955); "The *Sensus plenior* in the Last Ten Years," *CBQ* 25 (1963) 262–85; "The Problems of the *Sensus plenior,*" *ETL* 43 (1967) 460–69; "Hermeneutics," *NJBC* art. 79 §§49–51. Also J. Coppens, "Le problème du sens plénier," *ETL* 34 (1958) 5–20; repr. as *Le problème du sens plénier des Saintes Écritures* (ALBO 3/9; Louvain: Publications Universitaires de Louvain, 1958); P. Benoit, "La plénitude de sens des Livres Saints," *RB* 67 (1960) 161–96.

35. *The Interpretation,* 83; cf. JAF, *Text,* 130–31.

36. Ibid.

37. See *Decretum de Peccato Originali* of 17 June 1546, cap. 2 (DH 1512).

38. See n. 33 above.

39. See *AAS* 79 (1987) 380 (§17); *Origins* 16 (1986–87) 752; *The Pope Speaks* 32 (1987) 169.

40. See *Maria — Gottes Ja zum Menschen: Papst Johannes Paul II Enzyklika 'Mutter des Erlösers': Hinführung von Joseph Kardinal Ratzinger; Kommentar von Hans-Urs von Balthasar* (2nd ed.; Freiburg im B.: Herder, 1987) 107.

41. Dulles, *Craft of Theology* (n. 22 above), 85.

42. See further my *Scripture, the Soul of Theology* (n. 33 above), 78–80, 88, 96.

Chapter Seven: Raymond E. Brown, S.S., Renowned Representative of Biblical Scholarship

1. See pp. 5–6 above for a description of the content and effect of the encyclical.

2. (New York/Ramsey, NJ: Paulist, 1981).

3. (New York/Mahwah, NJ: Paulist, 1985).

4. See R. D. Witherup and M. L. Barré, "Biography and Bibliography of the Publications of Raymond E. Brown, S.S." in *Life in Abundance: Studies in John's Gospel in Tribute to Raymond E. Brown* (ed. J. R. Donahue; Collegeville, MN: Liturgical Press, 2005) 254–89.

5. *The Gospel according to John (i–xii)* (AB 29; Garden City, NY: Doubleday, 1966); *(xiii–xxi)* (AB 29A; 1970).

6. *The Epistles of John Translated with Introduction, Notes and Commentary* (AB 30; Garden City, NY: Doubleday, 1982).

7. *The Birth of the Messiah: A Commentary on the Infancy Narratives in Matthew and Luke* (Garden City, NY: Doubleday, 1977; New Updated Edition (ABRL; New York: Doubleday, 1993).

8. *The Death of the Messiah: From Gethsemane to the Grave: A Commentary on the Passion Narratives in the Four Gospels* (2 vols.; ABRL; New York: Doubleday, 1994).

9. *An Introduction to the New Testament* (ABRL; New York: Doubleday, 1997).

10. See K. Duffy, "The Ecclesial Hermeneutic of Raymond E. Brown," *Heythrop Journal* 39 (1998) 37–56.

11. E.g., *The Community of the Beloved Disciple* (New York/Ramsey, NJ: Paulist, 1979); *Antioch and Rome: New Testament Cradles of Catholic Christianity* (authored with John P. Meier; New York/Ramsey, NJ: Paulist, 1983).

12. Edited by B. Orchard et al. (London/New York: Thomas Nelson, 1953). It was meant to be the Catholic counterpart of another Nelson publication, the revised *Peake's Commentary on the Bible* (ed. M. Black and H. H. Rowley; 1963), in comparison with which it was sadly deficient. See the review of it by P. Benoit in *RB* 64 (1957) 598–601, esp. 600: "…une des caractéristiques de cet ouvrage: sa prudence très conservatrice."

13. R. E. Brown, J. A. Fitzmyer, and R. E. Murphy (eds.), *The Jerome Biblical Commentary* (2 vols. in 1; Englewood Cliffs, NJ: Prentice-Hall, 1968).

14. It was translated into Spanish in five volumes under the title *Comentario Bíblico "San Jerónimo"* (Madrid: Ediciones Cristiandad, 1971); and into Italian as *Grande Commentario Biblico* (Brescia: Queriniana, 1973). There was also a British imprint of the *JBC* published by Geoffrey Chapman of London (1968).

15. R. E. Brown, J. A. Fitzmyer, and R. E. Murphy (eds.), *The New Jerome Biblical Commentary* (Englewood Cliffs, NJ: Prentice Hall, 1990). This too has been translated into Italian under the title, *Nuovo Grande Commentario Biblico* (Brescia: Editrice Queriniana, 1997). A spin-off of the *NJBC* was *The New Jerome Bible Handbook* (London: Chapman, 1992), produced in England for use by students on the secondary school level. It is distributed in the U.S.A. by Liturgical Press, Collegeville, MN.

16. See the *Annuario Pontificio* (1973) 1036. The reaction to his appointment in the United States called forth many unfavorable criticisms. E.g., "Bible Group Gets Brown Hair Shirt," *Catholic Currents* (15 August 1972) 7; see further pp. 110–13.

17. See "Litterae apostolicae motu proprio datae: De Pontificia Commissione Biblica ordinanda novae leges statuuntur: *Sedula cura,*" *AAS* 63 (1971) 665–69 (cf. *EB* §§722–39; Béchard, *SD*, 147–50).

18. See pp. 110–30.

19. *The Status of the Nicene Creed as Dogma of the Church* (Washington, DC: National Catholic Welfare Conference, 1965).

20. *One Baptism for the Remission of Sins* (Lutherans and Catholics in Dialogue 2; ed. P. C. Empie and W. W. Baum; New York: U.S.A. National Committee for the Lutheran World Federation; Washington, DC: National Catholic Welfare Conference, 1966), esp. 9–21, 23–26.

21. *The Eucharist as Sacrifice* (Lutherans and Catholics in Dialogue 3; New York: U.S.A. National Committee for Lutheran World Federation; Washington, DC: United States Catholic Conference, 1967). The only paper by a Catholic biblical scholar was "Propitiation," by J. D. Quinn (pp. 37–44).

22. *Eucharist and Ministry* (Lutherans and Catholics in Dialogue 4; same publishers, 1970). See "Ministry in the New Testament," by J. D. Quinn (pp. 69–100).

23. *Papal Primacy and Universal Church* (Lutherans and Catholics in Dialogue 5; Minneapolis, MN: Augsburg Publishing House, 1974).

24. R. E. Brown, K. P. Donfried, and J. Reumann (eds.), *Peter in the New Testament: A Collaborative Assessment by Protestant and Roman Catholic Scholars* (Minneapolis, MN: Augsburg; New York: Paulist, 1973; London: Chapman, 1974). The participating scholars were: P. J. Achtemeier, M. M. Bourke, P. S. Brown, R. E. Brown, J. A. Burgess, K. P. Donfried, J. A. Fitzmyer, K. Froehlich, R. H. Fuller, G. Krodel, and J. Reumann.

25. See *Petrus in het geloof van de ionge kerk* (Bruges: Desclée de Brouwer; Boxtel: Katholieke Bijbelstichting, 1976); *Saint Pierre dans le Nouveau Testament* (Lectio divina 79; Paris: Editions du Cerf, 1974); *Der Petrus der Bibel: Eine Ökumenische Untersuchung* (Stuttgart: Calwer Verlag/Katholisches Bibelwerk, 1976); *Pietro nel Nuovo Testamento* (Rome: Edizioni Borla, 1988); *Shin-yakuseisho ni okeru Pe-te-ro* (Tokyo: Seibunsha, 1977); *Pedro en el Nuevo Testamento: Un trabajo en colaboración por autores Protestantes y Católicos* (Colección "Palabra Inspirada" 15; Santander: Editorial Sal Terrae, 1976).

26. R. E. Brown, K. P. Donfried, J. A. Fitzmyer, and J. Reumann (eds.), *Mary in the New Testament: A Collaborative Assessment by Protestant and Roman Catholic Scholars* (Philadelphia, PA: Fortress; New York: Paulist; London: Chapman, 1978). The participants were: P. J. Achtemeier, M. M. Bourke, R. E. Brown, S. Brown, K. P. Donfried, J. A. Fitzmyer, K. Froehlich, R. H. Fuller, G. Krodel, J. L. Martyn, E. H. Pagels, J. Reumann.

27. It appeared in a German translation as *Maria im Neuen Testament: Eine Gemeinschaftsstudie von protestantischen und römisch-katholischen Gelehrten...* (Stuttgart: Katholisches Bibelwerk, 1981); in Italian as *Maria nel Nuovo Testamento: Una valutazione congiunta di studiosi protestanti e cattolici* (Orizzonti biblici; Assisi: Cittadella Editrice, 1985); in Spanish as *Maria en el Nuevo Testamento* (Salamanca: Sigueme, 1982); and in a Japanese version (Tokyo, 1977).

28. I had earlier served for a term of five years on the International Dialogue set up by the Vatican Secretariat for Promoting Christian Unity and the Lutheran World Federation from 1967 to 1971. That Dialogue produced the pioneer document *The Gospel and the Church* (see H. Meyer [ed.], *Evangelium–Welt–Kirche* [Frankfurt am M.: O. Lembeck/J. Knecht, 1975), which has often been called "the Malta Report."

29. R. E. Brown, "The Unity and Diversity of New Testament Ecclesiology," *Novum Testamentum* 6 (1963) 298–308.

30. See *Baptism Eucharist and Ministry* (Faith and Order Paper 111; Geneva: World Council of Churches, 1982), formulated at Lima, Peru, in January 1982. Cf. *Baptism Eucharist and Ministry 1981–1990: Report on the Process and Response* (Faith and Order Paper 149; Geneva: World Council of Churches, 1990).

31. "Cardinal Mahony Calls Scripture Scholar's Death 'Great Loss,'" *Catholic News Service* (12 August 1998) 10.

32. Quoted in the archdiocesan newspaper, *Tidings*, 4 April 1980.

33. Published by Servant Books of Ann Arbor, MI, in 1983.

34. See "Present Imperfect," *Triumph* 8/7 (July 1973) 8. The editor was Michael Lawrence; senior associate editors, Leo Brent Bozell and Frederick Wilhelmsen.

35. This was a reference to an article written by M. Miguens, O.F.M., "Apostolic Succession? Fr. Brown's Inquiry," *Triumph* 7/4 (April 1972) 20–24, 42. Miguens was then a NT professor at the Catholic University of America, Washington, DC.

36. "The Bible Truth," *Triumph* 8/9 (November 1973) 8.

37. E.g., R. E. Burns, "The Brown Controversy," *The Wanderer* 113/17 (24 April 1980) 2 (objected to the Los Angeles Archdiocese's defense of Brown and of his talk at the CCD Congress in Anaheim, 6–9 March 1980); "Some Modernist Errors," ibid., 113/22 (29 May 1980) 2 (compares Brown's view on the infancy narratives with the condemned proposition 18 of the *Syllabus of Modernist Errors*); "Guardians of Orthodoxy," ibid., 113/39 (25 September 1980) 2; "Demythologizing Scripture," ibid. 115/22 (3 June 1982) 2; "The Beloved Disciple," ibid., 115/52 (30 December 1982) 2 (Brown as an example of "the Modernists today"); "A Reply to Bishop Hughes," ibid. 116/6 (10 February 1983) 2 (Burns denies that he ever "called Fr. Brown a heretic," but then compares Brown with Tertullian, "one of the greatest minds in the early church, [who] ended his days in the Montanist Heresy").

38. E.g., J. B. Carol, "The Deleterious Influence of Fr. R. Brown," *The Wanderer* 106 (29 November 1973) 1, 6 ("To sum up, Fr. Brown's theories...cannot...be reconciled with the authentic and constant teaching of the Catholic Church...what he has to offer concerning the human knowledge of Christ may be properly styled as neo-Modernism pure and simple").

39. E.g., S. Interrante, "Orange Diocese Laity Protest Fr. Brown Appearance," *The Wanderer* 113/4 (24 January 1980) 1, 6; "The Aftermath of Fr. Raymond Brown in Orange," ibid. 113/5 (31 January 1980) 7.

40. E.g., W. H. Marshner, "Heretics and Buffoons Meet in Washington," *The Wanderer* 106 (15 March 1973) 6; "Raymond Brown and the Charge of Modernism," ibid. 106/45 (15 November 1973) 1.

41. A. J. Matt, Jr., "Why Is Fr. Brown Afraid of Jerry Cal?" *The Wanderer* 109/19 (6 May 1976) 4.

42. E.g., F. Morriss, "The Evil Fruit of Fr. Brown's 'Scholarship,'" *The Wanderer* 111 (9 March 1978); "Fr. Brown Fathers Wild and Irresponsible Speculation," ibid. 111 (6 April 1978). See also his article, "Raymond Brown–Maritain: Gap Is Wide One," in *Catholic Northwest Progress* [Seattle] (11 May 1973) 4 ("Maritian [sic] died leaving among his last major works an expose [sic] of the vacuity and deceptiveness of the school of non-thought Father Brown represent [sic]").

43. E.g., J. J. Mulloy, "The 'Vilification' of Fr. Raymond Brown," *The Wanderer* 110 (13 January 1977) 1–2; "The Bible, the Magisterium, and Father Brown," ibid. 110 (2 February 1977) 1–3; "Fr. Brown on the Historical 'Truth' of the Gospels," ibid. 110 (10 March 1977) 1–2; "A Jew of the First Third of the First Century," ibid. 110/29 (21 July 1977) 1, 6–7; "Archbishop Whealon's Defense of Raymond Brown," ibid. 110 (25 August 1977) 4; "Fr. Brown's Ecumenism and the Primacy of St. Peter," ibid. 111(12 January 1978) 5; "Hans Kueng: The Doctrinal Image of Fr. Raymond Brown," ibid. 113/3 (17 January 1980) 4 (editorial); "How Eccentric Can a 'Centrist' Theologian Be?" ibid. 114/2 (4 June 1981) 4 (editorial); "The Cardinal's Critique of Fr. Brown's Scholarship," ibid. 113/9 (28 February 1980) 4, 6.

44. E.g., C. R. Pulver, "The Continuing Mis-Adventures of Fr. Raymond Brown," *The Wanderer* 106 (4 January 1973) ("Giddy perhaps from his recent appointment to the Pontifical Biblical Commission, this highly-touted Biblical scholar proceeded to behave in a most unscholarly manner. His address on December 3rd [in Syracuse, NY, Diocese] to over 400 priests and Religious of the diocese will surely go on record as one of the worst assaults on the Magisterium within recent memory"); "The Make-Believe World of Fr. Raymond Brown," ibid. 106 (7 June 1973) 9; (21 June 1973); 106/30 (2 August 1973) 4; "How Fr. Brown Stole Christmas," ibid. 109/7 (12 February 1976) 1, 6; "Fr. Raymond Brown Favors 'Centrist' Theology," ibid. 114/19 (7 May 1981) 3; "Can Fr. Brown Steal the Center?" ibid. 114/19 (7 May 1981) 4 (editorial).

45. E.g., P. H. Hallett, "The Infant and the Herods," *National Catholic Register* (12 December 1971): "the ultraliberal professor…brings into question the Virgin Birth. This is no surprise to those who know the works of this Modernist.…Is it uncharitable to suspect that those who would like to fictionalize the Infancy Narratives have a secret death-wish against the Divine Child? But He will always escape them, as He escaped the forces of Herod"; "Challenge of the Rev. R. E. Brown," ibid. (17 June 1973): on Brown's address, "The Crisis of Theology," to the NCEA; "Heresy Must Hurt," ibid. (9 September 1973) 4 ("the modernist doctrines of Father Raymond E. Brown"…How can Modernists like the Rev. R. E. Brown occupy posts on such vital organs of the Magisterium as the Pontifical Biblical Commission? He was appointed to the Commission in 1972, after his views on the Virgin Birth were already notorious"); "The Modernist Test," ibid. (6 January 1974) 4; "Rules for Bible Critics," ibid. (10 February 1974); "Fr. Brown Mispresents Bible, Catholic Church," ibid. (30 November 1975): on Brown, *Biblical Crises Facing the Church*; "Archbishop Dwyer Letter Makes History Expose," ibid. (24 April 1977): "Father Raymond Brown (notorious for unsound Biblical exegesis) has even been invited to Rome to lecture to Bishops. This, Your Holiness, is a scandal to many…."); "Criticizing the Critics," ibid. (15 June 1980), 537.

46. E.g., W. G. Most, "Believing Scriptures: Escape from Confusion," *National Catholic Register* (7 October 1973): claims Brown holds "There can be no miracles"; "Will Fr. Brown Be Next?" ibid. (20 April 1980): compares Brown to Leonardo Boff and asks, "Will R. Brown be the next on the carpet?"

47. See F.-M. Braun, *The Work of Père Lagrange* (Milwaukee: Bruce, 1963); *Père Lagrange: Personal Reflections and Memories* (New York: Paulist, 1985) 106–19; B. Montagnes, *Le Père Lagrange (1855–1938): L'exégèse catholique dans la crise moderniste* (Paris: Cerf, 1995). Cf. L.-H. Vincent, "Le Père Lagrange," *RB* 47 (1938) 321–54; (in English) "Père Lagrange," *Blackfriars* 19 (1938) 397–411, 474–86; also J. Murphy-O'Connor, *The École Biblique and the New Testament: A Century of Scholarship (1890–1990)* (Novum Testamentum et Orbis Antiquus 13; Göttingen: Vandenhoeck & Ruprecht, 1990) 6–9.

48. M.-J. Lagrange, *La méthode historique, surtout à propos de l'Ancien Testament* (Paris: Lecoffre, 1903; edition augmentée, 1904; reprinted with an introduction by R. de Vaux as *La méthode historique: La critique biblique et l'Église* [Paris: Cerf, 1966]); in English, *Historical Criticism and the Old Testament* (London: Catholic Truth Society, 1905).

49. See "Decretum de quibusdam rei biblicae commentariis in Sacra Seminaria non admittendis," *AAS* 4 (1912) 530–31. This decree was issued specifically against an OT introduction written by K. Holzhey, but it included a vague statement about writings of "similar spirit" of P. Lagrange ("ceu scripta plura P. Lagrange"), without further specification.

50. Delattre wrote *Autour de la Question Biblique: Une nouvelle école d'exégèse et les autorités qu'elle invoque* (Liége: Dessain, [1904]). To this criticism Lagrange replied in a pamphlet entitled *Eclaircissement sur la Méthode Historique: A propos d'un livre du R. P. Delattre, S.J.* (Paris: Lecoffre, 1905), which was printed in only two hundred copies and circulated privately, but never really published, because Lagrange's superiors counseled against publication of it. To it Delattre replied in turn in *Le Criterium à l'usage de la nouvelle exégèse biblique: Réponse au R. P. M.-J. Lagrange, O.P.* (Liége: Dessain, 1907); and again in an article, "Une lumière sous le boisseau," *Revue pratique d'apologétique* (1908), which also circulated in extract form *[non vidi]*.

51. See *The Interpretation*, 34; cf. JAF, *Text*, 26.

52. *The Wanderer* 131/36 (3 September 1998) 11.

53. Written by H. V. King, *The Wanderer* 131/37 (10 September 1998) 1, 11.

Chapter Eight: Concluding Remarks

1. San Francisco, CA: Harper & Row, 1989.
2. Grand Rapids, MI: Eerdmans, 2002.
3. *Nova et Vetera* 4/1 (2006) 12–32. In fact, Matera's article is only one of a symposium that deals with the book of Johnson and Kurz.

INDEXES

1. Index of Ancient Writings

A. Biblical Writings

B. Other Ancient Writings

2. Topical Index

Dumais, M., 132
Dupont, J., 120, 125, 129

Eliot, T. S., 74, 127, 130
Elliott, J. K., 133
Empie, P. C., 137

Farkasfalvy, D., 128
Fenton, J. C., 125
Fernández, A., 96
Fitzmyer, J. A., xi–xii, 59, 117, 125, 130–38, 141
Fogarty, G. P., 115
Fonck, L., 19–20
Foster, B. R., 131
Fowl, S. E., 125
Fragipane, D., 119
Freedman, D. N., xi, 103
Froelich, K., 137–38
Fryer, N. S. L., 126
Fuller, R. H., 137–38
Funk, R. W., 128

Galbiati, E., 31, 120
Galvin, J. P., 126
García Martínez, F., 132
Gnilka, J., 129
Gramont, S. de, 122
Grayson, A. K., 131
Greenfield, J. C., 131
Grelot, P., 134
Gross, W., 132
Grotefend, G. F., 80
Gunkel, H., 65

Hallett, P. H., 112, 140
Hallo, W. W., 131
Hamilton, G. J., 116

Hanson, A. T., 133
Harnack, A. von, 66
Hartlich, C., 127
Hasitschka, M., 133
Heidegger, M., 67, 128
Hincks, E., 80, 131
Hitchcock, J., 126
Holzhey, K., 141
Hooper, J. L., viii
Hummelauer, P. F. de, 21
Hünermann, P., xi

Interrante, S., 112, 139

James, N., 126
Jaspert, B., 128
John Paul II, Pope, 60, 98
Johnson, L. T., 115, 128, 142
Judd, R. H., 133

Käsemann, E., 109
Kasper, W., 59
Kegley, C. W., 128
Kelly, G. A., 111, 126
Kelly, J. N. D., 126
Kerrigan, M. P., viii
Kleinhans, A., 120
Krentz, E., 127
Krodel, G., 137–38
Kümmel, W. G., 123
Küng, H., 59, 71, 126–27, 140
Kurz, W. S., 115, 142

LaFontaine, R., 117
Lagier, C., 131
Lagrange, M. J., 21, 63, 113, 141
Lambdin, T. O., 103
Lawrence, M., 139